Simply
Dehydrated

Jenny Ross

Published by Choison Publishing Company

Design: Kristy Im and Shanna Joo
Editor: Kristy Im
Contributing Editors: Shanna Joo, John J.R. Lunasco, Jessica Song ,Crystal Tjen, and Elizabeth Yang
Main recipe photos: Fringe Photography, www.fringephotography.net
Additional photos: iStockphoto and Fotosearch
Food Styling: Jose Hernandez, Karina Kirk, and Jenny Ross

The information contained in this book is for informational purposes only and is not intended to diagnose, treat, or prevent any disease, symptom, or condition. Always consult your physician before making any changes to your diet and exercise regimen.

ISBN: 978-0-9859067-0-2

Printed in Hong Kong

1st edition, January 2013
10 9 8 7 6 5 4 3 2 1

Acknowledgements

I would like to thank the incredible team at 118 Degrees past and present for their continued support of our vision "To educate the world about the power of gourmet living foods." With special thanks to Kit, Jose, Karina, Alys, Alex, Taylor, Lisa, Tim, Concha, Lorenzo, Tino, Tamara, Matt, Leslie, Karen, and Dr. Kali. To my children Alysa and Dylan, thank you for your patience and for being the best teachers in my life.

Contents

Introduction

Dehydrating is a simple joy that allows us to enjoy delicious enzyme-rich foods with no preservatives. It creates a culinary option that we would not otherwise enjoy, without sacrificing some of the inherit health benefits of our food in the process of cooking. Dehydrating has become a way of life for many trying to avoid common food allergens, genetically modified foods and those enjoying an organic lifestyle. Whether you are dehydrating to make good use of leftovers or creating a delicious wrap or dessert, dehydrating allows you to create options that are easy to enjoy and store.

THE SIMPLE JOY OF DEHYDRATING

From a culinary perspective, dehydrating unlocks the door to fantastic, delicious, healthful treats of all kinds. In the dehydrator, a basic blend can become wraps, delicious breads, desserts and more. Soft fruits can become crispy treats and crunchy vegetables can become savory, soft fillings. Dehydrating allows you to be endlessly creative with the incredible gifts of mother nature and enjoy plant based foods in a whole new way.

To best describe it, dehydrating is like taking a prepared food item and placing it under the sun on a warm breezy day. The sun removes the moisture with indirect heat, along with the wind, leaving behind the essential food fibers and flavors, as well as the enzymes and nutrient value of the food. There is no applied heat so the food is naturally preserved with the nutrition intact.

Vibrant living is only a few steps away when you combine deliciously dehydrated staples with freshly made sauces and prepared fruits and vegetables. The dehydrator truly allows you to enjoy all natural, high nutrition foods in a fast and easy way.

WHAT DOES THIS MEAN FOR YOUR KITCHEN?

It is now easier than ever for you to create innovative food items from entrées and snacks, to pantry basics like wraps and breads, that are delicious, free of chemicals, and healthy for you and your family. You'll find expanded culinary options all throughout the book from marinated vegetables to soups and even salads that are enhanced by the basic principle of dehydrating.

THE BENEFITS OF DEHYDRATING

1. Preservative Free Foods: Preservatives are common ingredients found in the food products on the shelves of our marketplace, and inside restaurants world–wide, leading in many cases to diminished health and vitality. The dehydrator provides an easy and enjoyable alternative to foods prepared with preservatives. Everything from basic fruits and vegetables to advanced culinary dishes can be prepared in the dehydrator, preserving the food product while at the same time protecting your health from unnecessary additives.

2. Minimize Kitchen Waste: Kitchen waste is a natural by-product of a flourishing garden or even a busy week. As life gets more hectic we can find good uses for fruits, vegetables, sprouted nuts and seeds, even delicious sauces that would otherwise not be able to be preserved. In addition, nut pulps, vegetable fiber, and other by-products of juicing and blending can be used in dehydrated recipes! You will have no more waste, and instead, an abundance of healthy snacks!

3. Easy to create well-balanced allergen-free foods: The commercial processing of food and the modernization of agriculture has disrupted much of the natural benefits of the crops we enjoy. Many people are finding that they struggle with food allergies, which creates unwanted health issues in the body. In many cases, it's difficult to find foods in the market-place that are free of these common allergens. Dehydrating allows us to easily create gluten-free wraps, soy-free crackers, and many other delicious pantry basics and desserts, using the ingredients we choose and then save these items for use all month long. Balance can also be enhanced and maintained through these exciting culinary methods- it's easy to add in super foods, green foods, and additional protein to basic snacks like crackers and breads.

4. Active Enzyme Content of Foods: The more enzymes naturally present in foods, the easier it is for our body to begin the digestive process and find the necessary food sources of nutrition that all the vital systems of the body depend on. Eating a diet rich in enzymes leads to a vibrant lifestyle full of energy, clarity, and improved physical condition. When we dehydrate

foods, by removing the moisture without applying direct heat that will diminish the enzymes, we preserve many of the the nutrients for use by our body which leads to greater health for the holistic human.

5. Enhanced Nutritional Value of Foods: Food loses its volume of nutritional density the more we manipulate it. Everything from basic oxidation to the natural off-gasing of a fruit or vegetable once it has been picked, creates less of a nutrient dense food source for our bodies. Then when foods are heated above 118 degrees, especially oils, the food further breaks down and harmful toxins are created depending on the ingredients and cooking methods used. With dehydrating, we are able to prevent these processes from occurring and therefore enjoy foods with a superior nutritional value as often as possible. Another important benefit to note is the absence of food additives in homemade dehydrated foods.

6. Create Food in Large Batches For Quick and Easy Meals: Easy to create and store in large batches, dehydrating reduces kitchen time and gives you more time to enjoy those precious moments with family and friends. At first, it may seem like dehydrating takes longer, but really it creates freedom from making daily meals. With dehydrating it is easy to take time out once a week to create wraps, breads, crackers and mari-nated vegetables that you can enjoy, all week long by adding some fresh fruits and vegetables in five minutes or less. Less planning is needed once you get in the kitchen and get used to the process. Lots of creative expression can result from working with the simple mechanics of the dehydrator. It's simple to create food in large batches, with the dehydrator; just place the food in and walk away without worry. In addi-tion, most families report substantial financial savings once they begin to dehydrate on a regular basis!

Selecting a Dehydrator

There are two types of prominent dehydrators on the marketplace today, **(A)** Stacking dehydrators that heat from the bottom, or through a cylindrical tube that filters warm air through and over the stacked trays, and **(B)** Rectangular dehydrators with removable trays that are heated from behind with fans that circulate warm air over the food product on the stackable trays.

The Sedona is a rectangular dehydrator with removable trays. The basic unit has some great functional features that set it apart from other dehydrators in the same category. The Sedona's construction allows it to efficiently heat the food product with consistent overall coverage. These rectangular units, like the Sedona, are the best for living foods culinary preparations because they facilitate wraps, crackers and breads as well as optimize the surface area for dehydrating. Sensitive preparations like our coconut wraps or crepes cannot be accomplished in the stacking dehydrators.

Functionality is key when selecting dehydrators for the gourmet raw kitchen. The Sedona offers the living foods chef ultimate versatility and provides a dehydrating experience that is free of guesswork. All Sedona dehydrators feature the following basic options:

- **Easy read LED settings bar** with simple time and heat settings. This makes programming a snap. The Sedona also includes overheat protection ensuring that your living foods products do not heat up over the set temperature to maintain optimal enzyme activity, as well as the retaining of vital nutrients in your dehydrated products. You can easily set your desired temperature using increments of one, or take a shortcut and set your Sedona in increments of 10 to quickly get your dehydrator going. Then you can set the desired time so that you can walk away from your dehydrator and let it automatically turn itself off when your product is ready, or your can use the "continuous on" feature for up to 99 hours of dehydrating time.

- **Dual fans** circulate warm air over your dehydrated products allowing you versatility in your drying. This helps to maintain a consistent dying environment and also to alter the temperatures across two drying zones.

- **BPA-free tray and frame** construction allows you to rest easy ensuring no toxins will leach into your foods in the dehydrating process. In addition Tribest has created eco-friendly options with this dehydrator through its dual fan construction, allowing you to turn off a fan if only drying a tray or two to minimize electrical use. Your dehydrator will come shipped in recycled packaging as well instead of Styrofoam.

- **Transparent glass doors** allow you to view your product without having to open the door and affect the temperature inside your dehydrator.

The Sedona Combo has elaborated on these functional features to add even more benefit for the gourmet raw chef. Now when working with recipes that are sensitive and even more importantly where safe dehydrating it concerned you can have the added versatility of setting your dehydrator up to work for you.

THE SEDONA COMBO OFFERS UPGRADED FEATURES SUCH AS:

- **Dual Temperature and Dual Timer Setting**- "Fast" & "Raw" mode. For example, with the combo, you can set your dehydrator at the maximum temperature for us to 4 hours then have it automatically drop back down to 118 degrees or lower to finish the drying cycle. This is best for foods that need to have a higher heat in the beginning to ensure they do not ferment in your dehydrator. Most dehydrators take a few hours to actually heat up to 118 degrees inside, and the food product takes even longer to warm to that temperature since we are not using an applied heat like a stove. Please see page 22 for information on safe dehydrating techniques.

- **Debris Mat for easier cleaning**– The Sedona debris mat makes clean up easier and protects the construction of your dehydrator over long-term use. Also the debris mat doesn't take up a drying tray space. It is one extra tray to put at the bottom of the machine to cover it and collect any food debris that falls to the bottom of the machine.

- **LED lights in the back** for added visibility when opening and closing the dehydrator.

- **Detachable Display Panel**- If your machine malfunctions, the display panel with PCB board is now detachable with Sedona Combo for easier shipping and faster service. If any malfunction of the PCB is experienced, the customer doesn't have to send the whole machine back for repair or reprogramming.

- **Multi Lateral Air Flow Guide**- Sedona Dehydrators are more efficient in airflow distribution because of the dual fan technology, but recently we improved the airflow distribution system even more by adding the Multi Lateral Air Flow Guides. Before the airflow guide worked only parallel but now air is guided multi laterally; parallel and up & down.

- **Strengthened Door with Stainless Steel Handle and a Protection cover**- Stainless Steel Handle and Stainless Steel Protection cover makes it sturdier and nicer in appearance.

Some great recipes that make use of these added features include the Sedona wraps, marinated vegetables and fruit leathers of all types. Here are a few to get a jumpstart with the Sedona Combo:

High Protein Marinated Vegetables

MAKES 4 CUPS OF MARINATED VEGETABLES

For the marinade:

1   cup extra virgin olive oil

1   red bell pepper

1   clove garlic

1   Tbsp. curry powder, chili powder, or ground basil

1   Tbsp. raw agave or raw honey

For the vegetable mixture:

2   cups shiitake mushrooms

2   cups red chard or lacinato kale, chopped

2   cups peas or green beans

2   cups walnuts, sprouted

In a basic blender combine all marinade ingredients and blend well until a basic marinade is formed. This marinade can also be used as a salad dressing or garnish, and will save for up to 4 days in the refrigerator.

Prepare the vegetable mixture by tossing all ingredients in a large sized mixing bowl. Top the high protein vegetables with marinade and toss until well coated. Once coated, let it sit while

you prepare your dehydration tray. Line a dehydration tray with your choice of non-stick drying surface over a mesh screen. Transfer the contents of the mixture onto the tray and spread out evenly over the tray. Place the tray in the dehydrator and set on FAST mode at 155 degrees for 1 hour and RAW mode at 118 degrees for 30 minutes-1 hour. Then remove the vegetables and enjoy warm. Store leftovers in the refrigerator for up to 3 additional days, making sure to let cool before placing in the refrigerator. (*This recipe can also be made with the Sedona SD-P9000, pg. 170*)

Strawberry Wraps

6   **cups fresh strawberries**
4   **Tbsp. raw agave nectar**
½   **cup golden flax seeds or**
4   **Tbsp. psyllium husk**
1   **cup raw coconut flesh, cleaned**

Begin by first filling the blender with strawberries, agave, and coconut. Blend these into a basic purée. Then add in seeds or psyllium and blend again until a thick paste is formed.

Line 2 dehydration trays with a mesh screen and a non-stick drying sheet of choice. Then evenly spread mixture out over the trays evenly to create a thin layer about ⅛ inch thick. You should have a nice layer that you cannot see through on each tray.

Place dehydration trays in the dehydrator on FAST mode at 155 degrees for 1 hour and then set to RAW mode at 118 degrees for 2-5 hours until wrap is completely dry to the touch. Flip the non-stick drying sheet over and carefully pull back the wrap. Cut the wrap down into the portion sizes you will use to create your final dishes and store indefinitely in the refrigerator in an airtight container. *(This recipe can also be made with the Sedona SD-P9000, pg. 125)*

....

Overall, when selecting a dehydrator, remember that if it's a lifestyle change you are after that your tools can make all the difference in the world. Dehydrators make the possibilities of having allergen free wraps, healthy desserts and enzyme rich vegetable preparations possible, and not just possible, but fun! Dehydrating really does elevate the living foods kitchen to an art. I know you will love exploring these creative options using the functional Sedona dehydrator with your recipes.

SIMPLY DEHYDRATED

Dehydrating Basics

Dehydrating can be as simple as placing a piece of thinly sliced leftover apple in the dehydrator at 118 degrees and allowing it to stay there until completely dry.

Depending on what you are creating, there are different techniques to create culinary magic in the dehydrator. This book has been created to enjoy in sections depending on which of these techniques you are currently working with.

Here is a basic guide to the mechanics of dehydrating, the tools we often use in dehydrating and some simple guidelines to get you started. The more you work with your dehydrator the more you will become comfortable with the techniques that may be new to you. I encourage you to stick with the process. Overall, I find the dehydrator provides culinary freedom- no ovens or stoves to burn yourself on, no food is lost forever because you forgot a step-every part of dehydrating is ultimately forgiving; if you find a recipe is not working as you'd like you can consult the General Guidelines section of this book for ways to easily modify the food product and still enjoy it! Before I was an avid dehydrator I used to bake, so many cookies were lost burnt and charred with the best of intentions. When I first started dehydrating I was overwhelmed with soaking and sprouting and exact dehydration temperatures and times. I soon learned that because I was not using an applied heat that the temperatures, times and methods could all be altered to create my desired outcome. I am proud to say I have gone over

a decade without one burnt cake! At the same time I have enjoyed a decade of superior health and vitality, I have never felt better. I believe a big part of this is the ability to make fresh pure foods in my very own kitchen!

The dehydrator: The Sedona dehydrator is comprised of a basic box that heats the food products from inside using 2 fans, rotating air and heat. Consult your manual for specific guidelines for its operations, but for basic understanding this piece of equipment holds dehydration trays full of the foods you have created. The digital read-out allows for easy setting to 118 degrees or lower in most cases, and a timer. The equipment rotates warm air over your foods removing moisture, while the vents built into the front of the unit allows this moisture to escape.

Dehydration trays: The Sedona dehydrator comes with 9 BPA-free dehydration trays that easily slide in or out of the dehydrator. These trays can be easily cleaned with soap and water, or even in the dishwasher, as they are very durable.

Dehydration mesh screens: The Sedona dehydrator also comes with 9 BPA-free mesh screens that sit perfectly on top of the dehydration trays. Use a screen to line each tray. These screens make dehydrating foods fast and easy, and they provide support for other sheets, liners, and dishes that you may wish to place in the dehydrator. These can also be easily washed with soap and water or in the dishwasher.

Dehydration non-stick sheets: The Sedona dehydrator has a few different types of non-stick sheets that can be placed over the mesh screen on the tray. The sheets make working with mixtures, vegetables, and other items with more liquid run-off easy and helps to contain the food product itself. I recommend using non-stick sheets for everything from wraps, to lasagna, to marinated nuts and seeds. Typically we use the sheet for at least half of the drying time depending on the desired outcome. Parchment paper or basic saran wrap may be used in its place in some cases. These sheets also make clean up quick and easy!

Offset spatula and other spreading tools: I recommend an offset spatula to help evenly spread the batter for wraps and other food mixtures like crackers. Other spreading tools of different shapes and sizes like scrapers help to create a clean even spread of bread dough and desserts. Many mixtures designed for the dehydrator are rather sticky when first placed in the dehydrator and these basic tools will help make the job of getting your food creations into the dehydrator easy, clean, and fun.

Airtight containers: Once items have been fully dehydrated, many are shelf-stable as long as moisture does not reach them. We recommend storing your dehydrated foods in airtight glass containers for the best longevity. For the fresher items we create in the dehydrator, the same idea applies. Since the foods are preservative-free, glass airtight containers are the best to store these items in the refrigerator.

GENERAL GUIDELINES

When you prepare a fruit, vegetable mixture, or dessert for the dehydrator it's important to remember that since the dehydrator removes moisture the flavor will get stronger and the food items will diminish in size, meaning they will not be as thick, or will seem to shrink in the dehydrator.

Some items you place in the dehydrator may be very basic and you may not wish to add anything to enhance the flavor or texture. This is often the case with herbs, fruits, and vegetables that you'd like to dry out completely for indefinite storage.

You may consider even adding a bit of sea salt, lemon juice, or raw agave as a natural preservative and to bring out the inherit flavors of the food item.

Most recipes are going to follow some basic guidelines:

1. Prepare the food items, possibly tossing some soaked nuts with a marinade, blending up a batter for a wrap, or mixing a bowl of cracker ingredients.

2. Prepare a dehydration tray by setting the mesh screen on top. Depending on the mixture, it may be better to line the screen further with a non-stick sheet so the

excess moisture does not seep through the screen making a mess in the dehydrator or compromising the intended value of the recipe.

3. Place the tray in the dehydrator and adjust the dehydration settings for the temperature of choice and the time you'd like for the dehydrator to stop.

4. Once complete, you will remove the trays and remove the culinary treat you have created. In most cases you will enjoy some or all of it right away, in other cases you will choose to store it appropriately, either chilled or in an airtight container in your pantry.

Remember that your dehydrator is different from your oven, as it does not use an applied heat. Therefore, dehydrating times will vary from food item to food item and so will the flavor and texture of your culinary creations. Here are some tricks and tips to make some of the commonly found experiences easy to work with.

I have dehydrated my food item for the amount of time that it says but it still isn't dry? Since we are working with mother-nature, every plant strong recipe will be a little different. You may find your drying time will take longer or could even be shorter. This is especially true with items that are created to have a crunchy texture. It's fine to keep drying them until they are done as the desired outcome is a dry crunchy texture. To minimize the time, you may want to **(A)** flip the food item over so a different surface area is exposed, **(B)** if using a non-stick sheet you may want to remove the sheet half way through when the mixture is dry to the touch on the top, or **(C)** remove other items from the dehydrator and place the food item in the center of the dehydrator for maximum exposure to the fans moving the heated air.

I think the mixture I have created for a wrap/cracker or bread is too thin. What should I do? Many recipes that are used to create food products that we desire to stick together are made from flax or sprouted grains. Oftentimes they will thicken as they sit so you may wish to allow the mixture to sit for a few minutes and try spreading it again in a little bit. Another option if this doesn't work is to add a few tablespoons of ground flax or chia seeds. Both work as a natural thickening agent. Adding these to any of your mixtures a tablespoon at a time should not affect the flavor and allow the mixture to thicken up.

My fruits are changing color in the dehydrator? What does this mean? Fruits in particular, because of their natural sugar content, will get darker in the dehydrator. It is important that they do not turn black- see Safe Dehydrating section on page 22 for more information on this. In order to prevent discoloration you may elect to place a little lemon juice, raw honey, or agave

nectar on the fruit before drying. If you are using a marinade this will typically not occur as the marinade will act as a natural preservative in most cases.

My dehydrated crackers seem really oily, what happened? What about my marinated vegetables, they seem to have a lot of moisture? Oil becomes more viscous in the dehydrator and will spread out over drying surfaces. If your mixture has too much oil or perhaps the vegetable it was blended with was lower in fiber, there may be excess oil. The best thing to do would be to use a clean towel to absorb the excess oil and rotate the item you are drying. Marinated vegetables are the only exception to this rule as vegetables will sweat out their moisture and this will mix with any oily marinades. Simply pour off the excess liquid and continue to dry, the vegetables will likely absorb the remaining oils throughout the drying process.

I overdried my wraps and now they are crunchy instead of soft and flexible. Is there anything I can do? This is a common experience to have when you are getting used to the basics of creating soft wraps in your living foods kitchen. For a quick fix lay a clean damp towel over the top of your tray of wrap for 5-15 minutes, checking often. Remove and let air dry, the wrap should soften and then re-dry enough to prevent mold or bacteria growth.

My bread seems really thick and won't dry in the middle? Breads made using sprouted grains are very dense and should not be spread thick. The center of the bread can easily ferment and create harmful bacteria. The best thing to do is remove some of the dough and let dry again. As a rule of thumb, I usually remove the non-stick sheet half-way through drying breads and flip them over for even drying.

My dessert is really sticky? What happened? Sugars expand in the dehydrator, especially raw agave and honey. Sometimes if the recipe is not well enough combined, the moisture from the sweetener may not have properly absorbed into the fiber of the base of the recipe. Sometimes there may just be too much sweetener. I recommend removing the dessert and adding more of the base ingredient, to help absorb the sweetener and then placing back in the dehydrator. If you would prefer a cold dessert, you may freeze it as an adaptation of the dehydrated favorite.

My dehydrated cracker or vegetable has turned very dark almost black, is that ok?
In general, this type of discoloration is a sign of fermentation, as discussed in the next section, Safe Dehydrating. If you have a recipe that contains a fast fermenter you may need to pre-heat your dehydrator or place the dehydrator at a higher temperature for the first few hours to keep the temperature high enough to prevent fermenting. It is best not to use items that have discolored in this way.

Can I put sweets and savory items in the dehydrator at the same time? Yes, this is part of the joy of filling up the dehydrator and walking away coming back to all of your snacks done and ready to go! I recommend placing sweet items above the savory items, if you have transference from tray to tray it's a bit more forgiving. The only thing to note here are onions because they emit a very strong smell when dehydrating. Onions should be dehydrated in a room that is well ventilated, and when dehydrating onions, I typically only place savory items in the dehydrator.

SAFE DEHYDRATING

Overall the basics of dehydrating are pretty simple, but it's important to understand a few key concepts in safe dehydrating practices that will help prevent any adverse reactions to dehydrated foods:

1. Tomatoes and red bell peppers are fast fermenters! Therefore it's best to be sure to enjoy items like lasagna on the same day as it is dehydrated. Sometimes the tomatoes can ferment, tasting like a sharp zing on the tongue or like lemon. Tomatoes should be in the dehydrator 4-6 hours at most and should be kept at 118 degrees the entire time.

2. Pre-heating or heating at temperatures higher than 118 degrees is an acceptable way to help keep the food product itself at a higher temperature when working with fast fermenters or even marinated vegetables. Since we are not working with applied heat it will often times take at least 2 hours for the vegetables to even heat up to 118 degrees in these recipes. Setting your dehydrator at 155 degrees for the first 2 hours will speed up the process without cooking your food!

3. Cleaning is important in your dehydrator, especially removing any liquids once they accumulate to prevent the spread of mold or bacteria.

4. Sprouted grains are also quick to ferment, and it is important not to leave them more than 4-6 hours in the dehydrator. It is also recommended that they be kept at 118 degrees during the entire drying cycle and not to spread them more than ½ inch thick so that they may dry in the center. Most will be soft and flexible breads and should be refrigerated until use.

Breakfast Items

Easy Granola

Granola is a great staple to have in your pantry and is an item that you can pick up at a moment's notice. Using this basic recipe, you can add extra ingredients based on the flavors that you enjoy and what you may have already in your cupboard. This granola is also high in protein and a nutrient dense snack.

MAKES 2 TRAYS / ROUGHLY 4 CUPS WHEN DRIED

4   cups soaked and sprouted buckwheat groats (hulled, raw)*

½   cup raw agave, raw honey or maple syrup

½   cup sprouted seeds (choose sunflower, pumpkin, or flax)

1   Tbsp. cinnamon

1   tsp. nutmeg

1   tsp. sea salt

1   tsp. vanilla flavor or paste

In a large mixing bowl, begin by whisking together the sweetener of choice and all spices, including sea salt. Then make sure your buckwheat groats are well rinsed and cleaned. Toss in the buckwheat groats and seeds of choice. Add in any optional ingredients and toss well until entire mixture is well coated. Cover 2 dehydration trays lined with mesh screens and your choice of non-stick drying sheets, then pour bowl contents onto the tray, splitting evenly over the trays. Place in dehydrator set at 118 degrees for 6 hours. Then remove the non-stick sheet and continue drying at 118 degrees for an additional 4-6 hours until completely dry directly on the mesh screen. Store in an airtight container indefinitely.

* To properly soak and sprout the buckwheat simply rinse the buckwheat groats and place in mid-sized bowl. Cover the groats with clean water and let sit for 12 hours. The groats should become soft and a little sprout should begin. Rinse well and refrigerate before use. They should be used within 72 hours from the initial sprouting.

** Options that are fun to explore with this recipe include adding in fresh fruit sliced thinly, coconut, super foods of choice, dried fruits (recommend to reconstitute before drying in water) and other various nuts and seeds.

Sweet Corn Pancakes

Pancakes are known for the sweet aroma they provide throughout the house as they softly become ready for enjoyment. These delicious treats are exactly the same and are also rich in nutrition, flavor, and fun. These pancakes can be made and saved for up to 3 days. They are a crowd pleaser for sure so in our house we always make a double batch!

MAKES ROUGHLY 8 LARGE OR 12 SMALL PANCAKES

4 cups fresh corn kernels or 3 cups dried corn meal

2 cups fresh almond pulp or 1½ cups dried almond meal

1 cup ground buckwheat flour or coconut flour

½ cup raw honey, raw agave or maple syrup (1 tsp. Stevia may also be used in this recipe, but it is recommended to add ¼ cup additional liquids)

¾ cup almond milk, or coconut milk

2 Tbsp. fresh flax meal or psyllium husk

1 Tbsp. vanilla flavor or vanilla paste

3 fresh dates

1 tsp. sea salt

In a basic blender combine your choice of milk, sweetener, dates, vanilla, flax or psyllium, and sea salt. Blend until well combined. If using fresh corn, add the corn to a basic food processor and gently process with the s-blade until a coarse corn paste is formed. If using corn meal follow this same step but add ½ cup of the liquid to reconstitute the meal while in the food processor. Then in a large mixing bowl place the almond and flour of choice. Pour in the corn mixture, remaining liquid and toss together well using a spatula or a whisk; a thick paste should be formed.

Then line 2-3 dehydration trays with your choice of non-stick drying sheets. Begin scooping 4 Tbsp. of the batter onto the tray and press out into a circular pattern. Follow all across the tray and repeat until you have used all of the mixture. Place in the dehydrator at 118 degrees for 3-4 hours. You may flip the pancakes halfway through to diminish some of the drying time. Enjoy warm if possible with a little coconut butter and some delicious raw agave or maple syrup. Store the leftovers in the refrigerator and warm for 15 minutes in the dehydrator on high before enjoying!

Sweet Breakfast Bread

Sweet breads have been a tradition across many cultures as a breakfast item and can be enjoyed alone or with your favorite breakfast fruit or beverage. This sweet bread can be refrigerated for up to 7 days, making it a great recipe to make at the beginning of the week and use all week long.

MAKES 1 TRAY THAT CAN BE CUT TO MANY SIZES AND SHAPES

- 4 cups sprouted grain (rye, wheat berry, kamut or buckwheat)
- ½ cup ground flax, chia, or hemp seeds
- 4 fresh dates
- ⅓ cup raw sweetener of choice (for Stevia use 2 tsp.)
- 4 Tbsp. extra virgin cold pressed olive oil
- 2 Tbsp. raw almond butter
- 1 Tbsp. cinnamon
- 1 tsp. nutmeg or pumpkin pie spice (optional)
- 1 tsp. vanilla flavor or paste
- 1 tsp. sea salt

In a food processor, begin by combining the dates, olive oil, almond butter, and spices including sea salt. Then process the ingredients to a paste, using the s-blade. Follow this step by adding in the sprouted grain of choice and seed of choice. Process until well combined and grain has become well broken down. Then while processing, add the sweetener of choice until a dough ball begins to form. Line a dehydration tray with a mesh screen and your choice of non-stick drying sheet. Gently remove the dough ball from the food processor and press down the soft dough to cover the dehydration sheet. The mixture should make a rectangular shape between ¼ and ½ inch in thickness. Dehydrate at 118 degrees for 3 hours. Gently flip the bread and dehydrate again at 118 degrees for another 3 hours to make soft pliable sweet bread. Remove from the dehydrator once dry but not brittle (mixture should no longer be sticky at all). Refrigerate and use within 7 days. For best results warm with desired toppings in the dehydrator on high for 15 minutes before enjoying.

Fig Breakfast Bar

Figs are delicious, high in protein and potassium. These bars are perfect to take on the run and can be stored for up to 21 days or longer depending on your own preference for drying.

MAKES 16 BARS

- **8 cups dried mission figs or 6 cups fresh figs**
- **4 cups pecans or walnuts**
- **½ cup raw agave**
- **2 cups fresh apples or peaches, diced**
- **2 cups soaked and sprouted buckwheat groats (optional)**
- **2 Tbsp. cinnamon**
- **1 tsp. sea salt**

In a food processor with the s-blade attachment in place, process the pecans or walnuts into a meal and remove, set aside. Then place in the figs, spices, agave, and sea salt and process using the s-blade until thick paste forms. Then in a large mixing bowl combine all ingredients and fold together until well combined using a spatula. Line a dehydration tray with a mesh screen, covered with your choice of non-stick drying sheet. Then take the mixture and press out into a rectangular shape about ½ inch thick across the tray. Place in the dehydrator at 118 degrees for 4 hours. Flip the bars at that point directly onto the mesh screen and dehydrate another 4-6 hours until completely dry. If you choose to add the buckwheat, you will find it has become crunchy during the drying process and the rest of the bar remains somewhat soft. For additional protein, I suggest you add in your favorite super food protein mixture. Store in an air-tight container for up to 21 days or longer depending on how long you dry them.

Coffee Cake

This cake is a chai cinnamon swirl with that deep rich aroma of coffee. Coffee cake reminds me of all the cultures that have used coffee over the centuries in many forms as a way to connect with others and nourish their body and spirit in some way. Please enjoy this delicious treat all year round but particularly in the cold winter months over a sparkling fire with friends.

MAKES 6-8 SLICES

For the drizzle:

2 shots cold brewed espresso

½ cup agave nectar

3 Tbsp. almond butter

1 tsp. cinnamon

1 dash sea salt

2 drops coffee Stevia (optional)

For the cake:

3½ cups walnuts

2 cup soaked sprouted buckwheat or almond meal

⅓ cup agave nectar

1 Tbsp. pumpkin pie spice

1 tsp. cinnamon

1 tsp. sea salt

In a basic food processor with the s-blade attachment, gently process the walnuts to a meal and remove from the container. Then place in soaked buckwheat groats, all spices, and the sea salt. Process well and add in all but ½ cup of the walnut meal. Process briefly, and then add the agave nectar while processing until dough ball forms. Then remove the dough ball and refrigerate while making the drizzle. For the drizzle, blend all ingredients in a basic blender and refrigerate all but 4 Tbsp. Now take the dough ball and the drizzle and get ready to create the cake by lining a dehydration tray with a mesh screen and your choice of non-stick drying sheet. Then take the dough and gently press out a circular shape ½ - ¾ inch thick, 6-8 inches round. Take the remaining walnut crumble and place it over the top and then drizzle on the 4 Tbsp. of drizzle. Place the dehydration tray with the cake in the dehydrator at 118 degrees for 4 hours. Serve warm with fresh drizzle over each slice. Leftovers can be enjoyed for up to 4 additional days, when refrigerated.

Amazon Fruit Medley

This dish combines a delicious fresh fruit medley and a nutrient dense combination of delicious foods that together create a perfectly balanced breakfast. This breakfast looks lovely in a parfait dish and is fun to enjoy with family and friends on long weekends.

MAKES 1½ CUPS OF TOPPING AND 4-6 SERVINGS OF PARFAIT

For the medley:

2   kiwis

2   mangos

1   pineapple

2   cups other fresh seasonal fruit

For the amazon topping:

1   cup shredded coconut

1   Tbsp. maca root

4   Tbsp. almond or hemp butter

½   cup hemp seeds

½   cup cacao nibs

½   cup soaked date pieces

2   Tbsp. orange zest

1   tsp. vanilla flavoring

6   Tbsp. raw honey

4   Tbsp. bee pollen

First prepare the topping in the Sedona Dehydrator. Begin by pulsing all ingredients in a basic food processor with the s-blade attachment. Pulse ingredients until combined but not overly expressed, meaning that it does not become too sticky. Remove the mixture from the food processor and place directly on a dehydration tray lined with a mesh screen. Sprinkle out over the tray evenly for an even dry. Place in dehydrator at 118 degrees for 4 hours. Remove topping and store in an airtight container until ready for parfait.

To create the parfait:
Creatively slice all fruit to create different shapes and sizes. Layer in a parfait glass with 2 Tbsp. of amazon topping over each layer.

Chai High Protein Oats

Oats should be enjoyed raw after being soaked. I like to rinse mine and soak them in nut milk for better flavor and enjoyment. Make this bowl of oats 1 hour in advance while you are enjoying your morning routine and you will have a nice bowl of oats ready to take you through your morning with ease.

MAKES 2-4 SERVINGS

2-4 cups of raw oats, rinsed

2-4 cups almond milk (make fresh
   if possible)

2   Tbsp. nut butter of choice

4   Tbsp. raw agave, raw honey or
   2 drops of Stevia

2   Tbsp. cinnamon

2   tsp. pumpkin pie spice

1   dash sea salt

2   Tbsp. maca root (optional)

1   tsp. ginger juice (optional)

Begin by preparing oats, rinse them well and soak them in almond milk for 20 minutes (1 cup of oats will require 1 cup of milk). Then take the oats and whisk in all remaining ingredients. Separate into serving bowls, place the bowls on a dehydration tray and place inside the Sedona dehydrator. Set the dehydrator at 135 degrees for 1 hour and enjoy in 40 minutes to an hour. If you have more time, set the dehydrator at 118 degrees and leave for up to 2 ½ hours. Garnish the top with your favorite oatmeal fruits, nuts or even a sprinkle of granulated coconut sugar. Should be made fresh to enjoy, leftovers may be stored in the refrigerator for 48 hours.

Super Food Starter

Super foods are functional foods that lead to health and longevity by delivering a powerful punch in a small package. While your needs for super foods may change over the years based on your body's needs, this is a good grab and go snack that you should be able to enjoy all throughout the day.

MAKES 6 CUPS WHEN DRY

4   cups raw soaked nuts of choice
2   cups soaked goji berries
1½ cups cacao nibs
4   Tbsp. raw coconut oil or butter
2   Tbsp. greens powder of choice
2   cups fresh or dried figs (soaked in water), diced
1   cup fresh fruit of choice
3   Tbsp. raw agave, raw honey or 3 drops of Stevia
1   pinch sea salt

This simple recipe is fast and easy and can be in your Sedona in minutes! Simply toss together all ingredients in a large mixing bowl until all ingredients are coated in a light mixture of sweetener and oil. Line a dehydration tray with a mesh screen, covered with your choice of non-stick drying sheet and scoop out the contents of the bowl onto the sheet. Dehydrate at 118 degrees for 12 hours. Store indefinitely in an airtight container.

Buckwheat Breakfast Sandwich

Sandwiches are a nice way to combine multiple food groups for optimal nutrition. You get to enjoy the combined flavors of all the great ingredients inside, which is a unique taste experience in it's own right. We know for optimal health we must stimulate all the vital systems of the body especially as we get ready for a busy day, this sandwich does just that!

MAKES 4 SANDWICHES

For the omega-rich bread:

2   **cups ground raw buckwheat**

2   **cups hemp seeds**

2   **Tbsp. flax seeds**

1   **cup water**

½   **cup extra virgin olive oil**

1   **Tbsp. agave**

1   **tsp. cinnamon**

1   **tsp. sea salt**

1   **cup dried raisins soaked**

For the sandwich:

1   **mango**

1   **avocado**

2   **cups fresh spinach**

2   **cups assorted vegetables of choice**

2   **Tbsp. hemp butter, coconut butter, or other raw spread of choice***

First create the omega rich bread by combining the buckwheat, hemp seeds and flax seeds in a bowl. Toss together to combine. Then in a blender blend all remaining ingredients. Pour this mixture over the dry ingredients and fold both together until well combine using a spatula. Line 2 dehydration trays with mesh screens and press out 4 Tbsp. of the bread at a time into 4 inch round shapes, ¼ inch in thickness. Place these on the trays filling up the trays. Place the trays in the dehydrator and dehydrate these for 4 hours at 118 degrees. Remove these while they are still some-what soft, and refrigerate until use for up to 15 days.

To create the sandwiches slice the mango and avocado into lengthwise pieces. Begin by gently spreading the sandwich bread with a spread of your choice and then lay all ingredients and top with other slice of bread.

*Smashed avocado is actually my favorite as the spread and it's fast and easy. Enjoy fresh for best results.

Strawberry Crêpes

Crêpes are known to be light and fluffy and these are no different. This delicious combination is a great breakfast or even dessert for that matter and should be thoroughly enjoyed, as it is great for brain function, heart health, and also easy to digest.

MAKES 4 SERVINGS

For the crêpe wrap:

4   pieces Strawberry Wraps
    (pg. 125)

For the filling:

½   cup coconut butter

2   cups fresh coconut flesh, or 1
    cup raw macadamia nuts or
    raw cashews

½   cup coconut water, raw apple
    juice or purified water

½   cup raw agave, raw honey or
    4 drops Stevia

1   tsp. vanilla flavor or vanilla
    paste

4   cups fresh strawberries, diced

2   bananas

Orange zest for garnish

First prepare the filling by combining the coconut butter, nut of choice, water of choice, and sweetener of choice, with the vanilla and ½ cup berries in a basic blender. Blend well until a thick rich crème has formed. Cut down the banana either into small slices or diced,and add them into a mid-sized mixing bowl with the diced strawberries. Toss in the rich crème and make filling.

Place the wraps on the cutting board and fill with ½ cup of filling. Gently roll wrap around or fold over to create a crease. Then place the crêpe in the Sedona Dehydrator on a dehydration tray with the mesh screen in place. Dehydrate at 118 degrees for 45 minutes to an hour. Remove and tray, garnish with zest and possibly some shredded coconut. Leftovers should be refrigerated and enjoyed in 36 hours.

Caramel Pockets

Caramel is an inviting and warming flavor, it's great during the holiday season and is especially nice paired with a variety of fresh seasonal fruits.

MAKES 4 SERVINGS

For the wrap:

4   Simple Seed Wraps (pg. 116)

For the pocket filling:

4   Tbsp. raw almond butter

½   cup raw agave, raw honey
    or maple syrup

1   Tbsp. cinnamon

1   tsp. nutmeg or pumpkin
    pie spice

1   Tbsp. maca root

1   tsp. sea salt

4   cups seasonal fruit (delicious
    with apples, figs, pears,
    peaches and fuyu persimmons)

First create the filling by whisking together all filling ingredients, save the fruit in a small bowl. Then in a mid-sized bowl combine the sauce and the seasonal fruit after dicing the fruit to bite sized portions. Then on a cutting board line up all the wraps, split the filling evenly, piling in the center, over each wrap. Gently fold the corners of each wrap to the center creating a pocket. Gently place the pockets on a dehydration tray lined with a mesh screen. Place in the dehydrator at 118 degrees for 45 minutes to an hour. The edges of the wrap should be crispy and the filling nice and warm. Plate the dish and garnish with additional sweetener if desired. Leftovers should be refrigerated and enjoyed in 36 hours.

Fruit & Vegetable Basics

Spicy Pineapple

Growing up in Southern CA I was heavily influenced by the Latin flavors of nearby Mexico. This spicy pineapple recipe is fast and easy, and of course delicious with a kick. The warming spices make it a great treat year round, but especially in the winter time.

MAKES ROUGHLY 12-16 SLICES

1   whole large ripe pineapple

For the marinade:

½   cup extra virgin olive oil

2   Tbsp. lemon juice or lime juice

2   tsp. sea salt

4   Tbsp. raw honey or agave

1   tsp. sea salt

1   pinch cayenne pepper

Begin by slicing pineapple on the bias all the way down into ¼ inch ring sized pieces. The thinner the piece the faster it will dehydrate. Make sure not to exceed ½ inch in thickness for best results. Then in a basic blender combine the marinade ingredients and blend until well combined. In a large mixing bowl, toss together the pineapple and sauce until all pineapple pieces are well coated. Then line a dehydration tray with a mesh screen and your choice of non-stick drying sheet or parchment paper. Carefully lay out each slice one next to the other and repeat until all pineapple has been laid out. Dehydrate at 118 for 4 hours, then flip the pineapple and dry for another 4-8 hours. Store in airtight container indefinitely.

*One variation on this recipe that is nice is to simply dice the pineapple and follow the same steps, stopping after 6 hours of drying time to maintain additional moisture. These must stay refrigerated and used within 5 days but they make a great garnish for tacos, salads and more.

Cinnamon Pears

Pears are a delectable fruit, and this recipe is good with all types of pears from Asian to Bartlett to Bosc. Enjoy pears year-round now with the use of the dehydrator to make this tasty snack. This snack also makes a stunning garnish on top of salads and appetizer dishes when entertaining.

MAKES ROUGHLY 36 PIECES

6   fresh ripe pears

⅓   cup extra virgin olive oil

2   Tbsp. cinnamon

½   tsp. nutmeg

1   dash sea salt

1   tsp. agave nectar (optional)

First prepare 2-3 dehydrating trays with mesh screens and your choice of non-stick drying sheets. Then begin by slicing the pears thin- no smaller than ⅛ inch but no larger than ⅓ inch into uniform slices. In a basic blender continue the recipe by combining the other ingredients and quickly process until well combined. Pour the cinnamon marinade into a mid-sized tossing bowl, and with tongs, dip the pears one by one into the sauce and begin lining them up on the non-stick drying sheets. Once complete, place the trays into the dehydrator and set the dehydrator at 118 degrees. Dehydrate for 4 hours, and then gently flip the pears and dehydrate another 4-8 hours until dry and crisp. Store in an airtight container.

Apples Two Ways

Apples are a staple in your daily diet because they are so high in malic acid and key vitamins. Here is one recipe that can be enjoyed two different ways for a little variation on an old favorite. An apple a day really will keep the doctor away!

MAKES 1-2 TRAYS OF DICED SWEET SOFT APPLES AND 2-3 TRAYS OF APPLE CRISPS

4-6 Fuji, Gala, Red Delicious or Pink Lady Apples*

½ cup raw agave nectar, raw honey, or maple syrup

2 Tbsp. cinnamon

1½ tsp. pumpkin pie spice or nutmeg

1 tsp. sea salt

1 Tbsp. maca root (optional- adds a caramel flavor)

For both variations begin by combining marinade ingredients in a small bowl and whisking until well combined.

Diced Sweet Soft Apples:
For this variation dice all apples and combine in a large mixing bowl. Top with sauce and toss very well until all apples are well coated. Line a dehydration tray with a non-stick drying sheet on top of a mesh screen and top with apples. Apples should be stacked about 1 inch thick on the sheet. Place in dehydrator and set dehydrator at 118 degrees for 2 hours. Then quickly toss the apples again and dehydrate for an additional 1-3 hours depending on desired softness and moisture content. These apples are excellent when soft but still moist. They can be served on top of morning breakfast cereals, toast, ice cream, and more. Once dried to desired consistency, refrigerate immediately and enjoy within 4 days.

Apple Crisps:
For this variation prepare the apples by slicing thin with a food processor or a mandoline. Apples should be no thicker than ⅓ of an inch. Then in a large mixing bowl toss together with marinade until well coated. Next, line a dehydration tray with a mesh screen and your choice of a non-stick drying sheet. Then layout the apples so they are stacked on top of each other but no thicker than ½ inch. Place in the dehydrator set at 118 degrees for 4 hours. Remove the tray and invert onto another tray lined with only the screen the apples and continue dehydrating another 4-6 hours until completely dry. Pull the apples apart into sizes that best suit your needs and store in an airtight container indefinitely.

*Any apples can be used for this recipe, but tart varieties like Granny Smith are best.

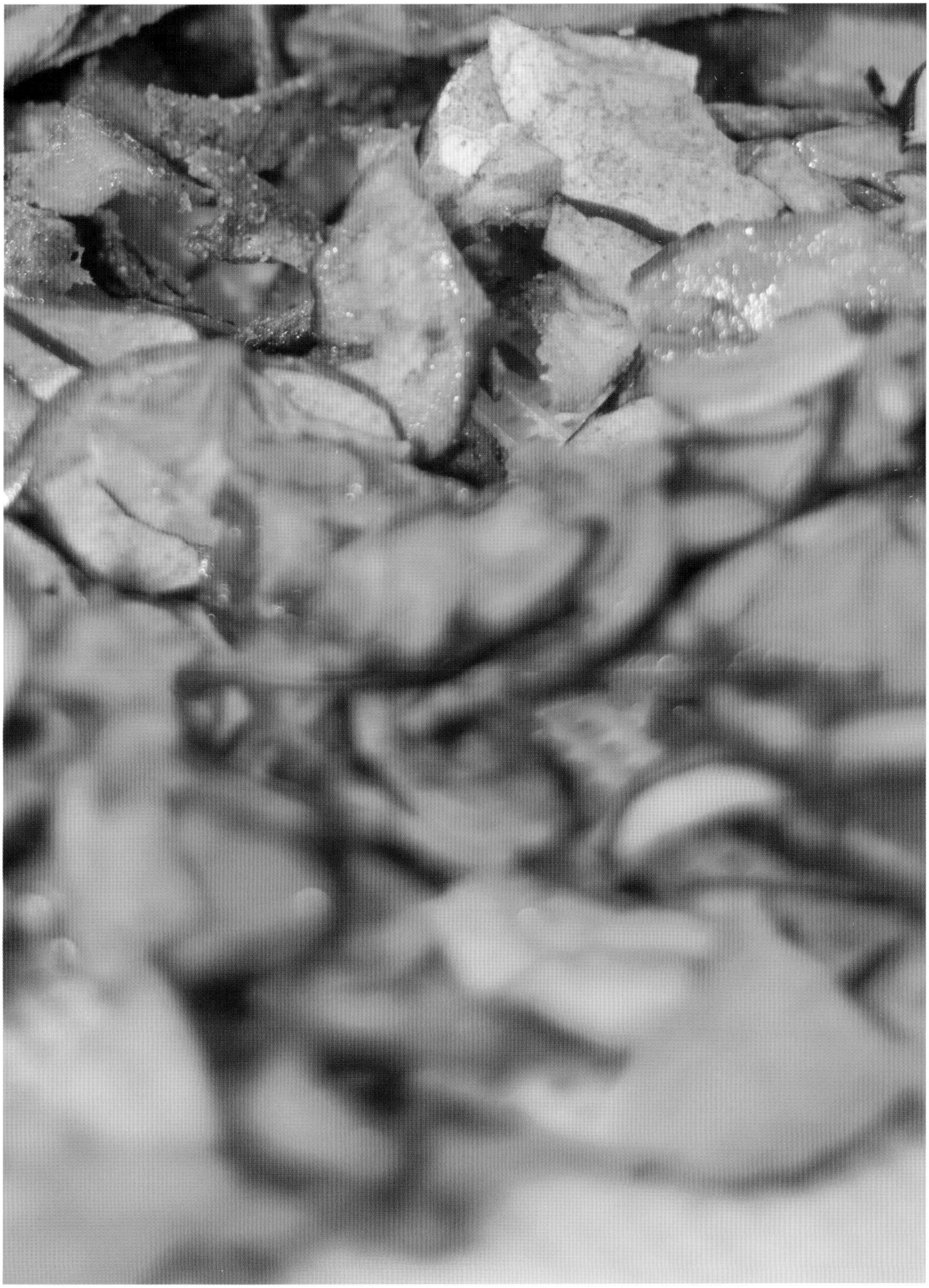

Persimmon Star Wheels

Persimmons are only in season a few short times out of the year, and many people remark how abundant they are during those times. This is a fun way to preserve your persimmons for enjoyment all year long. Not only are they delicious but fun especially for kids and curious family members as the pattern of the Fuyu persimmon makes a nice star shape. We affectionately call them "star crisps" at home!

MAKES 4 DOZENS

8	Fuyu persimmons
⅓	cup extra virgin olive oil
4	Tbsp. raw agave nectar
1	tsp. of lemon juice
1	pinch sea salt
1	vanilla bean* (optional)

Begin by simply whisking together the ingredients for the marinade. Then cut the persimmons on a bias, right through the center forming pieces that are ¼ inch in thickness. Then in a mid-sized mixing bowl toss the two together making sure the persimmon is well coated. Place directly on the dehydration tray lined with a mesh screen and place in the dehydrator at 118 degrees for 4 hours. For faster drying time, flip the persimmons and repeat.

Curried Mango

Curried Mango is fun to incorporate into any dish or to enjoy on its own. You can make this recipe unique to your own enjoyment by adding a spicier curry if you enjoy a spicy curry dish or a sweet curry to satisfy your sweet tooth. Either way the results are phenomenal.

MAKES ROUGHLY 12-16 SLICES

2-4 mangos of any variety

4 Tbsp. raw coconut oil

1 tsp. of lime juice

2 Tbsp. curry powder of choice

4 Tbsp. raw agave

1 tsp. vanilla paste (optional)

Begin by removing mango pits by carefully slicing the mango off of the pit on each side. Scoop out the soft flesh and slice into lengthwise pieces ⅓ inch thick. Then in a basic blender combine all marinade ingredients and blend on high until very well combined. Use a mid-sized bowl to toss together the marinade and the mango until the mango is well coated. Line a dehydration tray with non-stick drying sheet of choice and layout mango so they are not overlapping on the tray. Dehydrate at 118 degrees for 4 hours, then remove from the non-stick sheet and place the mangoes directly on the mesh screen until completely dry (estimated another 4-6 hours). Store in an airtight container, indefinitely.

BBQ Coconut Jerky

Fresh coconut makes a delicious jerky when properly dried and is an invaluable source of essential fatty acids. Your brain and your heart will thank you if you pack this tasty treat to nourish you for your next big outdoor adventure.

MAKES 1 FULL TRAY

2   cups young Thai coconut flesh (mature coconut may be used as well)

¼   cup coconut water
4   Tbsp. coconut oil
1   chipotle pepper
2   Tbsp. raw honey or raw agave nectar
2   Tbsp. chili powder
1   tsp. sea salt

Begin by making sure that all coconut flesh is clean and well prepared to slice down into desired size. Remember that as you dry the coconut it will further diminish in size by ⅓. Cut down the cleaned coconut to desired shape and size. Then in a basic blender combine all marinade ingredients and blend on high until very well combined. Toss together the marinade and the coconut pieces. Line a dehydration tray with your choice of non-stick drying sheet and pour contents of bowl onto the sheet. Place in dehydrator at 118 degrees for 4 hours. Then gently flip the mixture onto the screen itself and dehydrate an additional 4-6 hours or until completely dry. Store in an airtight container, indefinitely.

Squash Sticks

These are fun to look at and make a crunchy snack that can be enjoyed year round and they are especially great for kids. The marinade is light and flavorful and the squash itself is an excellent source of fiber even when dried. Using yellow crookneck squash and green zucchini in combination will lead to a fun and colorful collection of vegetable snacks.

MAKES 2 TRAYS

4   squash

1   red bell pepper
¼   cup extra virgin olive oil
1   sun dried tomato
4   Tbsp. water
1   tsp. sea salt
1   tsp. chili powder, 1 tsp. curry powder, or 1 tsp. dried Italian seasoning (optional)

Prepare squash by removing the ends. Using a mandoline, slice the squash lengthwise ¼ inch in thickness and place in a midsized mixing bowl. Then in a basic blender combine all marinade ingredients and blend well until a nice rich thick paste is formed. Pour this over the squash in the mixing bowl and carefully toss well until all squash is well coated. Then line a dehydration tray with a mesh screen and your choice of non-stick drying sheet. Line up each squash piece side by side but not overlapping. Place in dehydrator at 118 degrees for 3 hours. Then gently remove the sticks from the non-stick drying sheet and place them directly on the screen to dry the rest of the way, another 4-6 hours. They should be crunchy and completely dry to the touch. Store in an airtight container, indefinitely.

Italian Eggplant

Eggplant is a staple in many Mediterranean cultures due to its consistency and unique ability to transform into a variety of flavorful dishes. This combination is a delicious snack on top of any fresh salad or by itself and will surely make you dream of a Tuscan village in the countryside!

MAKES 3-4 TRAYS

2   large eggplant (Japanese eggplant may be substituted)

1   cup fresh chopped parsley or basil (or try both!)

1   cup extra virgin olive oil

1   Tbsp. sea salt or Himalayan salt

2   cloves garlic

Prepare the eggplant by removing the stem and the end. Begin by slicing the eggplant from end to end creating round medallions no thicker than ⅓ inch. Then in a basic blender combine the marinade ingredients, save the fresh herbs and blend well. In a large mixing bowl place the eggplant and the fresh chopped herbs. Toss this together first. Then add the marinade a little at a time, tossing vigorously in between so that the eggplant may absorb the marinade a little at a time. Let sit for ½ hour, so the eggplant may absorb the flavor of the marinade. While the mixture sits prepare a dehydration tray by lining it with a mesh screen and pre-set dehydrator at 118 degrees to allow the machine to pre-warm for best results. Then line the tray with the medallions next to each other but not overlapping. Place in the dehydrator at 118 degrees for 6-10 hours until completely dry. For a more chip-like consistency cut the eggplant no thicker than ¼ inch and add 4 Tbsp. additional olive oil to the bowl when tossing. Store in an airtight container, indefinitely.

Tomato Pepper Triangles

Tomato and red bell peppers come together once or twice a year as a perfect seasonal pair. This creates the perfect opportunity to seize the moment to create a snack that can be enjoyed all year long. Great as a garnish, topping, alone, or even as a light crust- this snack is easy to prepare and packs a flavorful punch.

MAKES 2 TRAYS

4   Roma tomato (suggested, any tomato can be used)

3   large red bell peppers

For the marinade:

½   cup extra virgin olive oil

⅓   cup water or coconut water

4   Tbsp. dried Italian seasoning or ¼ cup fresh basil

2   Tbsp. raw agave or raw honey (dates may also be used)

4   cloves garlic

1   Tbsp. sea salt

Begin by slicing 2 of the 3 red bell peppers very thin and placing in a large sized mixing bowl, followed by 2 roma tomatos. Then in a basic blender combine all marinade ingredients and blend well. Add in the remaining tomato and red bell pepper and purée until a thick red paste is formed. Gently pour the paste over the thinly sliced vegetables and toss mixture vigorously. Line 2 dehydration trays with your choice of non-stick sheets over the mesh screens. Divide the mixture evenly and spread out to ¼ inch thickness. Place in dehydrator at 118 degrees for 4 hours. Then invert the mixture to remove from non-stick sheets and place directly on the dehydration tray with mesh screens, dry another 4 hours at 118 degrees until completely dry. Cut down into triangular pieces. Store in an airtight container indefinitely.

Sweet Onions

Onions are plentiful year-round in most areas and finding a great recipe for the abundance of onions in your kitchen can prove to be a challenge. This is a great way to preserve them naturally and also spice up your entrées in a hurry. When dehydrating onions it is important to remember the smell and flavor will intensify as they dry. As a result we recommend placing the dehydrator in a room with a good amount of ventilation while drying these tasty treats.

MAKES 4-6 CUPS

6   onions of any type (sweeter
     varieties are delicious in this
     recipe)

For the marinade:

½   cup extra virgin olive oil

¼   cup raw agave or raw honey

1   Tbsp. sea salt or Himalayan salt

¼   cup fresh parsley*, 2 cloves
     garlic, or 2 Tbsp. chili powder
     (optional)

Carefully and quickly remove the onion skins and slice down into very thin rings roughly ⅛ inch to ¼ inch in thickness. Place onion slices in large mixing bowl covered in water with a pinch of salt. Then in a blender combine marinade ingredients* and blend well. Drain the salt water from the onions and replace with the marinade. Let sit refrigerated for 1 hour. Line 2-3 dehydration trays with mesh screens and your choice of non-stick drying sheet and pre-set the dehydrator to 118 degrees to pre-warm for best results. Then place the onions over the non-stick sheets and place in the dehydrator at 118 degrees for 4 hours. Invert the onions and place directly on the dehydration screen. Dehydrate until completely dry another 4-6 hours. Gently pull apart onions and store in an airtight container indefinitely. These onions will be soft when fully dry with just a little crunch.

*When using chopped parsley do not blend in but fold into onion mixture instead.

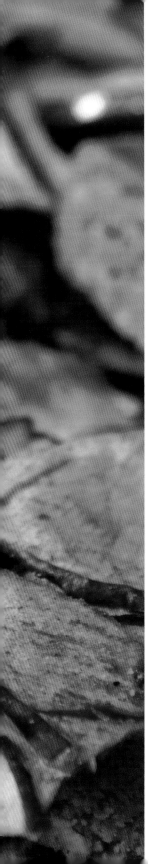

Crackers &
Crunchy Snacks

Vegetable Crackers

Working with vegetable fibers to create a cracker is an excellent way to use your juice pulp leftovers. I recommend not using the pulp of celery or cucumbers but most other commonly juiced varieties like carrots, beets and greens work very well in this recipe.

MAKES 2 TRAYS

2   cups vegetable pulp

2   cups ground flax seeds
     (suggest to use golden flax) or
     4 Tbsp. ground chia seeds and
     2 cups ground sunflower seeds

1   cup purified water

4   sun dried tomato halves

3   Tbsp. ground basil

2   Tbsp. extra virgin olive oil

2   cloves garlic

1   Tbsp. sea salt

Begin by grinding the flax seed or sunflower seeds 2 cups at a time, in a dry blender and transfer to another bowl until ready to create the full recipe. Then in a high-power blender combine first the spices, tomato and the water and blend until well combined. In a large sized mixing bowl combine then all the ingredients and toss until very well combined, the mixture should be a thick paste.

Line 2 dehydration trays with your choice of non-stick drying surface and split the mixture evenly over both trays. For best results use a rolling pin or even your hands to spread the mixture out evenly. The longer the mixture sits the thicker it will become so it is recommended to use it promptly.

Place the trays in the dehydrator at 118 degrees for 2 hours. Remove the trays and flip the mixture directly onto the screen. Score the mixture at this point to create your own desired shape and then place the trays back in the dehydrator and dehydrate at 118 degrees an additional 8 hours or until completely dry. You may want to sprinkle additional spices over the top of the cracker before placing in the dehydrator for even more flavor.

Remove the crackers when completely dry from the dehydrator and store in an airtight container indefinitely.

Spice of Life Crackers

One of the keys to success with crunchy snacks in the Sedona is to keep in mind that the flavor will become more intense in the dehydrator as the recipe dries. If you love a full range of flavor this cracker is for you, it's definitely a great companion to hummus of any kind or a delicious pesto.

MAKES 2 TRAYS

4   cups ground flax seeds
    (suggest using golden flax)
2   cups purified water
1   zucchini

2   Tbsp. Italian seasoning
1   Tbsp. sea salt
1   tsp. mustard powder
1   tsp. onion powder
1   tsp. garlic powder or 1 clove
    fresh garlic
1   tsp. cumin

Begin by grinding the flax seed, 2 cups at a time, in a dry blender and transfer to another bowl until ready to create the full recipe. Then in a high-power blender combine first the spices, zucchini and the water and blend until well combined. Then add the flax seeds and blend until the mixture is thick but still pourable.

Line 2 dehydration trays with your choice of non-stick drying surface and split the mixture evenly over both trays. For best results use an offset spatula to spread the mixture out evenly. The longer the mixture sits the thicker it will become so it is recommended to use it promptly.

Place the trays in the dehydrator at 118 degrees for 2 hours. Remove the trays and score the mixture at this point to create your own desired shape and then place back in the dehydrator at 118 degrees and dehydrate an additional 8 hours or until completely dry. You may want to sprinkle additional spices over the top of the cracker before placing in the dehydrator for even more flavor.

Remove the crackers when completely dry from the dehydrator and store in an airtight container indefinitely.

Simple Sedona Flax Crackers

Toss and go with this simple recipe that requires very little prep time. Make these crackers your own using the suggested additions in the recipe.

MAKES 2 TRAYS

4   cups flax seeds (soak for 1 hour prior to use in 6 cups of water)

2   cups sliced vegetable leftovers (recommend tomato, red bell pepper, or squash)

4   Tbsp. desired seasonings, dried or fresh (recommend basil or a spice blend)

1   Tbsp. sea salt

Begin by soaking and rinsing the flax seed, transferring to a mid-sized mixing bowl for the recipe preparation. Then add in all ingredients and toss together well until all ingredients are thoroughly dispersed throughout the recipe mixture. The flax should be thick and very moist.

Line 2 dehydration trays with your choice of non-stick drying surface and split the mixture evenly over both trays. For best results use an offset spatula to spread the mixture out evenly over the trays. The longer the mixture sits the thicker it will become so it is recommended to use it promptly.

Place the trays in the dehydrator at 118 degrees for 2 hours. Remove the trays and score the mixture at this point to create your own desired shape and then place the trays back in the dehydrator and dehydrate at 118 degrees an additional 8 hours or until completely dry. You may want to sprinkle additional spices over the top of the cracker before placing in the dehydrator for even more flavor.

Remove the crackers when completely dry from the dehydrator and store in an airtight container indefinitely.

Buckwheat Thins

Buckwheat is a gluten-free grain that is very high in protein. This base is excellent to use for several types of snacks and these buckwheat thins make a great pantry staple. Kids love them too!

MAKES 2 TRAYS

2 cups ground flax seeds (golden flax suggested)

2 cups sprouted buckwheat

2 cups purified water

2 red bell peppers

1 tsp. onion powder

1 tsp. garlic powder or 1 clove fresh garlic

1 tsp. cumin

Begin by grinding the flax seed in a high-power blender and transfer to another bowl until ready to create the full recipe. Then in a high-power blender combine first the spices, red bell pepper and the water and blend until well combined. Then add the flax seeds and buckwheat and blend again until the mixture is thick but still pourable.

Line 2 dehydration trays with your choice of non-stick drying surface and split the mixture evenly over both trays. For best results use an offset spatula to spread the mixture out evenly. The longer the mixture sits the thicker it will become so it is recommended to use it promptly.

Place the trays in the dehydrator at 118 degrees for 2 hours. Remove the trays and score the mixture at this point to create your own desired shape and then place the trays back in the dehydrator and dehydrate at 118 degrees an additional 8 hours or until completely dry. The other option with this recipe would be to start off by creating round shapes or other shapes you may enjoy and then flip the shapes halfway through the drying process. (This may require use of additional trays). You may want to sprinkle additional spices over the top of the cracker before placing in the dehydrator for even more flavor.

Remove the crackers when completely dry from the dehydrator and store in an airtight container indefinitely.

Onion Poppy Seed Crackers

Onion Poppy Seed Crackers are a European tradition and this variety is a high protein blend of plant strong ingredients that are perfectly paired with vegetable toppings of all sorts.

MAKES 3 TRAYS

2   **cups ground flax seeds (golden flax suggested)**

2   **cups ground buckwheat flour or sprouted quinoa**

½   **cup ground chia seed**

4   **Tbsp. poppy seeds**

1   **red onion, sliced thin**

2   **cups purified water**

3   **tsp. onion powder**

½   **tsp. cracked caraway seeds**

1   **tsp. garlic powder or 1 clove fresh garlic**

1   **tsp. sea salt**

Begin by grinding the flax seed in a high-power blender. Then in a large mixing bowl combine the flax, buckwheat or quinoa, poppy seeds and chia seed. Toss together lightly and add in the thinly sliced red onion. Now using tongs toss these ingredients vigorously until well combined. Then in a high-power blender combine the spices and the water and blend until well combined. Pour this mixture over the onion mixture and toss together well.

Line 3 dehydration trays with your choice of non-stick drying surface and split the mixture evenly over all 3 trays. For best results use an offset spatula to spread the mixture out evenly. The longer the mixture sits the thicker it will become so it is recommended to use it promptly.

Place the trays in the dehydrator at 118 degrees for 2 hours. Score the mixture at this point to create your own shape and then dehydrate an additional 8 hours or completely dry. You may want to sprinkle additional spices over the top of the cracker before placing in the dehydrator for even more flavor.

Remove the crackers when completely dry from the dehydrator and store in an airtight container indefinitely.

Kale Crunchers

Kale is an important part of a plant strong diet because it is so rich in nutritional value, protein especially. This is a great use of kale that needs to be used a great way to get your kale year round anywhere. It's a slightly spicy mixture so it packs a great punch of flavor!

MAKES 3 TRAYS

8   cups of thinly sliced kale, stems removed (recommend Lacinato kale)

4   cups ground flax seeds (golden flax suggested)

2   cups purified water

1   Roma tomato

1   red bell pepper

1   chipotle pepper

1   Tbsp. chili powder

1   clove garlic

4   Tbsp. extra virgin olive oil

1   Tbsp. sea salt

Begin by cleaning the kale and removing the stems. Chop the kale down to thin ribbon like pieces of kale and place in a large sized mixing bowl. Then follow this by grinding the flax seed 2 cups at a time in a dry blender and transfer to another bowl until ready to create the full recipe. Then in a high-power blender combine water, vegetables and all spices and blend until well combined. Then add the flax seeds to the blender and blend until mixture is thick but still pourable. Pour the mixture over the kale pieces and toss together very well until all of the kale is well coated. Kale should begin to absorb the mixture and shrink down in size.

Line 3 dehydration trays with a mesh screen with your choice of non-stick drying surface and split the mixture evenly over all 3 trays. For best results use an offset spatula to spread the mixture out evenly, the mixture should be no thicker than ¼ inch. The longer the mixture sits the thicker it will become so it is recommended to use it promptly.

Place the trays in the dehydrator at 118 degrees for 10 hours. Remove the mixture from the non-stick sheets and cut down to the desired size. Place back on the dehydration trays and dehydrate the crunchers again at 118 degrees an additional 1-2 hours or until completely dry. You may want to sprinkle additional spices over the top of the crunchers before placing in the dehydrator for even more flavor.

Remove the crackers when completely dry from the dehydrator and store in an airtight container indefinitely.

Yam Chips

Yams are a great source of iron and potassium so having this crunchy chip around is good for your health for sure! You may add your own spice combination to this chip before or after the drying process. I do recommend trying them first as a basic recipe, as most yams are intensely flavorful. They are fantastic dipped in mustard and ketchup and a fun side dish to serve up.

MAKES 4-6 CUPS

4   large yams, peeled and sliced
     very thin

1   cup extra virgin olive oil
3   Tbsp. raw agave or raw honey
2   Tbsp. sea salt

Prepare the yams and let sit in the refrigerator 4-8 hours. In a basic blender combine marinade ingredients and blend until well combined. Place the yams in a mid-sized mixing bowl and pour marinade over the yams. Let the final mixture of yams and marinade sit for around 4 hours.

Line 3 dehydration trays with a mesh screen and your choice of non-stick drying surface and split the mixture evenly over all 3 trays. For best results make sure the yam pieces are not overlapping as you spread them over the trays.

Place the trays in the dehydrator at 118 degrees for 4 hours. Then remove the trays and remove the non-stick surface, transferring the yams straight onto the mesh screen on the trays. You may want to sprinkle additional spices over the top of the cracker at this point before placing back in the dehydrator for even more flavor. Place the trays back in and dehydrate the yams until completely dry (roughly another 6 hours).

Remove the chips when completely dry from the dehydrator and store in an airtight container indefinitely. You may enjoy misting these with fresh cold pressed olive oil and sprinkle with spices before enjoying.

Butternut Crunch

Butternut squash is a delicious winter squash that creates a lusciously sweet crunchy treat. You can cut these to any shape you'd like but I strongly recommend a thin stick that you can enjoy on top of your pasta dishes or alongside a salad or small rounds for dipping.

MAKES 2 TRAYS

1½ cups golden flax seeds
4   cups cubed butternut squash
2   cups purified water

2   Tbsp. rosemary
3   cloves garlic
4   Tbsp. extra virgin olive oil
1   Tbsp. chili powder
1   Tbsp. sea salt
1   tsp. raw gave nectar or raw honey

Begin by grinding the flax seed in a dry blender and transfer to another bowl until ready to create the full recipe. Then in a high-power blender combine first the spices and the water and blend until well combined. Then add the squash to the blender, blending well until a purée is formed. Add then the flax seeds to the blender and blend until a thick mixture is formed that is still pourable.

Line 2 dehydration trays with your choice of non-stick drying surface and split the mixture evenly over both trays. For best results use an offset spatula to spread the mixture out evenly over the trays. The longer the mixture sits the thicker it will become so it is recommended to use it promptly.

Place the trays in the dehydrator at 118 degrees for 2 hours. Remove the trays and score the mixture at this point to create your own desired shape and then place the trays back in the dehydrator and dehydrate at 118 degrees an additional 8 hours or until completely dry. You may want to sprinkle additional spices over the top of the cracker before placing in the dehydrator for even more flavor.

Remove the crackers when completely dry from the dehydrator and store in an airtight container indefinitely.

Walnut Kris-Cross

This rich brain booster is high in Vitamin A and E as well as essential fats. These crunchy snacks are good alone or with a dip. Try them with some whipped garlic for a fun flavor combination.

MAKES 2 TRAYS

4   cups walnuts

½   cups purified water

4   Tbsp. cold pressed extra virgin olive oil

3   stalks celery

2   Tbsp. Italian seasoning

1   tsp. mustard powder

1   tsp. onion powder

1   tsp. garlic powder or 1 clove fresh garlic

1   tsp. cumin

First process the walnuts in the food processor, using the s-blade attachment, down to a meal. In a basic blender combine the celery, water, oil and spices and blend well. Turn the food processor back on and begin adding to the mixture from the blender until both are now well combined in the food processor. Process further until dough ball forms.

Line 2 dehydration trays with mesh screens and your choice of non-stick drying surface and split the mixture evenly over both trays. Press out into desired shapes, I love to use cookie cutters here creating stars, hearts and fun animal shapes to attract the eye of the kids for a healthy treat. You may even want to sprinkle on some flake sea or river salt here for more of a salty flavor profile.

Place the trays in the dehydrator at 118 degrees for 4 hours. Remove the non-stick drying sheets and place the Walnut Kris-Cross directly on the mesh screens for an additional 6 hours until dry and crumbly.

Remove the crackers when completely dry from the dehydrator and store in an airtight container indefinitely.

Fruit Crisps

Fresh fruit is important to use right away so this recipe is a great opportunity to make use of fruits that may be ready to use and in abundance in your kitchen. The following recipe is a recommendation but it works well with fruit of all types as long as they have enough available fiber to bind the recipe.

MAKES 2 TRAYS

4   **cups mango, diced**
2   **cups pineapple, diced**
1   **cup papaya, diced**
½   **cup ground chia seed or hemp seed**

4   **Tbsp. agave nectar**
1   **Tbsp. vanilla bean paste**
1   **tsp. sea salt**

Begin by pulsing the fruit in a food processor with the s-blade attachment until well combined and broken down but not a liquid. Then add in the chia or hemp to the food processor and allow to sit for a few minutes, so the seed may absorb the excess moisture. Then turn on the processor and add the remaining ingredients while it is processing stopping as the mixture is clearly well combined.

Line 2 dehydration trays with mesh screens and your choice of non-stick drying surface. Using a tablespoon or ice cream scoop, scoop 2 Tbsp. of the mixture at a time onto the sheets leaving space to flatten. For best results use an offset spatula to spread the mixture out evenly into rounds. The longer the mixture sits the thicker it will become so it is recommended to use it promptly.

Place the trays in the dehydrator at 118 degrees for 4 hours. Remove the trays and remove the non-stick drying surfaces and transfer the crackers directly onto the mesh screen and place back in the dehydrator at 118 degrees for 8 additional hours.

Remove the crackers when completely dry from the dehydrator and store in an airtight container indefinitely.

Mushroom Crisps

Dried mushrooms have a strong flavor and these are perfect on a crudités platter or as a starter base for delicious appetizers to share.

MAKES 2 TRAYS

- 4 cups sliced shiitake or cremini mushrooms
- 1 cups ground flax seeds (golden flax suggested)
- 6 Tbsp. ground chia seeds (optional, may use more flax if desired)

- 2 cups purified water
- 1 zucchini
- 6 Tbsp. cold pressed extra virgin olive oil
- 1 Tbsp. miso paste
- 1 tsp. garlic powder or 1 clove fresh garlic

- ⅛ cup chopped basil or parsley

Begin by grinding the flax in a dry blender and transfer to another bowl until ready to create the full recipe. Then in a high-power blender combine first the garlic powder, olive oil, miso, zucchini, and the water and blend until well combined. Then add the flax seeds and chia seeds to the blender, blending until thick but still pourable. In a large mixing bowl combine the mushrooms, blended mixture, and basil or parsley and fold together. Further toss the mixture together until the mushrooms are well broken down by the mixture to very small pieces.

Line 2 dehydration trays with a mesh screen and your choice of non-stick drying surface. Using a tablespoon or ice cream scoop, scoop 2 Tbsp. of the mixture at a time onto the sheets leaving space to flatten. For best results use an offset spatula to spread the mixture out evenly into rounds to form the crisps. The longer the mixture sits the thicker it will become so it is recommended to use it promptly.

Place the trays in the dehydrator at 118 degrees for 4 hours. Then remove the trays and remove the non-stick drying surfaces, transferring the crackers directly onto the screen and placing back in the dehydrator at 118 degrees for 8 additional hours.

Remove the crackers when completely dry from the dehydrator and store in an airtight container indefinitely.

Breads

Breads are a delightful treat to have in your pantry at all times. Sandwiches, appetizers, pizzas and more can be made within minutes if you have these breads ready to go.

Simple Sprouted Bread

This is a basic recipe to use as a starter, by adding your own desired flavors like olive, basil, or sun-dried tomato you can create a multitude of delicious options to share with your family and friends.

MAKES 2 TRAYS

- **4 cups sprouted rye or wheat berries**
- **⅓ cup cold pressed extra virgin olive oil**
- **1 tsp. sea salt**
- **2 Tbsp. seasoning of choice or 2 cloves garlic**

Begin by rinsing the sprouted grains well. Then prepare the food processor by setting up the s-blade attachment. Place the grains in the processor with the salt and seasoning of choice and process until well masticated. Then add in the olive oil while the grains are processing from the top of the food processor. Stop when a dough ball begins to form.

Bread of this type can now be placed on a non-stick drying sheet in any shape you choose. To keep it simple, I recommend splitting the mixture evenly on 2 dehydration trays lined with non-stick drying sheets. Carefully press out the dough over the tray until evenly dispersed. The dough should be about ¼ inch thick at this point.

Place the dehydration tray into the dehydrator at 118 degrees for 4 hours. After 4 hours, remove the tray and flip the bread over straight onto the dehydration tray. Place back in the dehydrator at 118 degrees for another 1-2 hours. Remove the bread while still pliable yet not wet to the touch. Store this bread in an airtight container in the refrigerator for up to 14 days, after cutting down into desired shape.

Parisian Breadsticks

Garlic and basic cheese combined in this delightful version of delicious breadsticks, create a flavor that is universally enjoyed. The Parisians pride themselves on social eating and this is definitely a recipe you will love to share.

MAKES 8 BREADSTICKS

2   cups Simple Sprouted Bread dough (pg. 80)

⅓   cup cold pressed extra virgin olive oil

½   cup Everyday Cheese (pg. 133)

½   cup fresh basil

¼   cup diced garlic cloves

1   tsp. sea salt

Begin by rinsing the sprouted grains well. Then prepare the food processor by setting up the s-blade attachment. Place the simple sprouted dough in the processor with the salt and 2 Tbsp. of diced garlic and process until well combined. Then in a small mixing bowl toss the remainder of the diced garlic, the basil, the "Everyday Cheese" and the olive oil together. Separate the dough into 8 even sized portions and press out on a cutting board covered in saran wrap or your choice of non-stick surface into a 2 inch by 4 inch rectangular shape about ¼ inch thick. Evenly disperse the savory topping over each piece down the center lengthwise and roll into breadstick shape.

Place the breadstick directly on the screen of a dehydration tray and place the breadsticks in the dehydrator at 118 degrees for 3 hours. Gently flip the breadsticks and place back in the dehydrator at 118 degrees for an additional 2 hours.

Enjoy these breadsticks fresh out of the dehydrator. Leftovers may be stored in the refrigerator in an airtight container for 2 additional days.

Sedona Foccacia

Flat flavorful foccacia bread makes an excellent high protein companion to any meal. Enjoy this alone or with your favorite salad.

MAKES 2 TRAYS

4 cups Simple Sprouted Bread dough (pg. 80)
⅓ cup cold pressed extra virgin olive oil
1 cup sun-dried tomato, soaked
2 cups thinly sliced red onions
2 cups Kalamata olives
1 Tbsp. sea salt
2 Tbsp. Italian seasoning

Prepare the food processor by setting up the s-blade attachment. Place the dough in the processor with the salt, ¼ cup of sun-dried tomato, and ⅛ cup diced olives. Process briefly until mixture is well combined. Line 2 dehydration trays with mesh screens and your choice of non-stick drying surface.

Begin spreading the dough out over the 2 non-stick drying sheets covering the mesh screens, splitting the mixture evenly over both. Carefully press out the dough over the tray until evenly dispersed. The dough should be about ¼ inch thick at this point. Toss together the remaining ingredients in a small mixing bowl and split the mixture evenly over each tray and gently press into the dough.

Place the dehydration tray in the dehydrator at 118 degrees for 4 hours. After 4 hours remove the tray and transfer the bread over straight onto the dehydration tray. Place back in the dehydrator at 118 degrees for another 1-2 hours. Remove the bread while still pliable yet not wet to the touch. Store this bread in an airtight container in the refrigerator for up to 5 days, after cutting down into desired shape.

Burnt Orange Yam Bread

This is gluten-free bread that is soft and pliable, it makes the perfect bun! It's also a good source of Vitamin A and Iron.

MAKES 2 TRAYS

4   cups peeled yams, diced

2   cups ground buckwheat flour

4   Tbsp. golden flax seeds

⅓   cup cold pressed extra virgin olive oil

1   tsp. sea salt

2   Tbsp. chili powder

Begin by dicing and preparing the yams. Then prepare the food processor by setting up the s-blade attachment. Place the yams in the processor with the salt and seasoning and process until well masticated. Then add in the olive oil while the yams are processing from the top of the food processor. In a separate small bowl whisk together the buckwheat flour and the flax seeds. Then turn the processor back on and then begin adding the yam mixture and continue until well combined. Let it sit 20 minutes before pressing out to allow mixture to thicken.

Bread of this type can now be placed on a non-stick drying sheet in any shape you choose. Carefully press out the dough over a dehydration tray lined in your choice of non-stick surface until you achieve the desired shape. The dough should be ¼ inch thick at this point.

Place the dehydration sheet in the dehydrator at 118 degrees for 4 hours. After 4 hours remove the tray and flip the bread over straight onto the dehydration tray. Place back in the dehydrator at 118 degrees for another 1-2 hours. Remove the bread while still pliable yet not wet to the touch. Store this bread in an airtight container in the refrigerator for up to 14 days, after cutting down into desired shape.

Honey Date Bread

There are a couple great options for this bread depending on your needs and food choices. This bread may be enjoyed as a grain-free alternative or with your choice of sprouted grain. The honey dates are a delicious combination particularly with the stronger flavor of grains like rye.

MAKES 2 TRAYS

4   cups sprouted rye or wheat
    berries or 4 cups almond meal
1½ cups honey dates
2   Tbsp. cinnamon
1   cup purified water
1   tsp. sea salt

Begin by rinsing the sprouted grains well or removing any large pieces from almond meal. Then prepare the food processor by setting up the s-blade attachment. Place the grains in the processor with the salt and cinnamon and process until well masticated. Or if using the almond meal, process the spices and meal lightly. Then in a basic blender lightly blend the dates with water until a thick paste or chutney like mixture is formed. Now add this mixture to the remainder of the dough while processing in the food processor until a dough ball forms.

The honey date bread can now be placed on a non-stick drying sheet in any shape you choose. To keep it simple, I recommend lining 2 dehydration trays with mesh screens and non-stick drying sheets, splitting the mixture evenly over both. Carefully press out the dough over the tray until evenly dispersed. The dough should be about ¼ inch thick at this point.

Place the dehydration sheet in the dehydrator at 118 degrees for 4 hours. After 4 hours remove the tray and flip the bread over straight onto the dehydration tray. Place back in the dehydrator at 118 degrees for another 1-2 hours. Remove the bread while still pliable yet not wet to the touch. Store this bread in an airtight container in the refrigerator for up to 14 days, after cutting down into desired shape.

Nutty Bread

Nutty breads are a great high-energy snack and should be enjoyed throughout the day to maintain clarity and receive a healthy dose of vitamins and minerals.

MAKES 1 FULL TRAY

2   cups sprouted buckwheat

2   cups walnut pieces, soaked

⅓   cup cold pressed extra virgin olive oil

2   Tbsp. orange zest (optional)

2   Tbsp. raw honey (optional)

1   tsp. sea salt

First take half of the walnuts and process them to a meal in the food processor with the s-blade attachment in place. Then follow this by rinsing the sprouted buckwheat well. Place the buckwheat in the processor adding to the walnut meal with the sea salt and seasoning of choice and process until well masticated. Then add in the olive oil while the grains are processing from the top of the food processor. Stop when a dough ball begins to form. Now add in the remaining walnuts and pulse until chopped to form chunks throughout the dough.

Line a dehydration tray with a mesh screen and your choice of non-stick drying surface. Carefully remove the dough from the processor and press out the dough over the tray until evenly dispersed. The dough should be about ½ inch thick at this point.

Place the dehydration sheet in the dehydrator at 118 degrees for 4 hours. After 4 hours remove the tray and flip the bread over straight onto the dehydration tray. Place back in the dehydrator at 118 degrees for another 1-2 hours. Remove the bread while still moist yet not sticky. Store this bread in an airtight container in the refrigerator for up to 14 days, after cutting down into desired shape.

Quinoa Rounds

Quinoa is an excellent source of protein. It is a gluten-free seed and is a fun ingredient to work with that is an important source of nutrition at the same time. It is considered a complete protein with a full chain of amino acids, as well as a great source of daily fiber and magnesium.

MAKES 2 TRAYS

- 4 **cups sprouted quinoa**
- 2 **cups vegetable pulp (carrots and beets are best)**
- 1 **zucchini**
- 1 **cup water**
- ½ **cup ground flax seeds or chia seeds**
- 2 **cloves garlic**
- 2 **Tbsp. seasoning of choice**
- 1 **tsp. sea salt**

First blend the zucchini, water, and seasoning in a basic blender. Follow this by rinsing the quinoa well. Then prepare the food processor by setting up the s-blade attachment. Place the quinoa in the processor with seed of choice and vegetable pulp and process until well masticated. Then add in the mixture from the blender while the grains are processing from the top of the food processor. Stop when a dough ball begins to form.

Line 2-3 dehydration trays with your choice of non-stick drying surface covering the mesh screens. Then scoop out 3 inch balls of the dough evenly across the screen and press down with the back of a spoon into even rounds about ⅓ inch thick.

Place the dehydration sheet in the dehydrator at 118 degrees for 4 hours. After 4 hours remove the tray and flip the bread over straight onto the dehydration tray. Place back in the dehydrator at 118 degrees for another 1-2 hours. Remove the bread while still pliable yet not wet to the touch. Store this bread in an airtight container in the refrigerator for up to 14 days, after cutting down into desired shape.

Coconut Crisp Bread

This is a fusion recipe that is really fun to prepare and creates a delicious aroma while drying. It's great to share as sweet bread on a dessert tray and makes very nice breakfast bread as well.

MAKES ROUGHLY 12 COCONUT CRISP BREADS

- 2   cups pecan meal
- 2   cups buckwheat flour or 2 cups sprouted wheat berries
- ⅓   cup olive oil
- 2   cups shredded coconut
- ½   cup date paste
- 2   tsp. sea salt

Prepare the food processor for use with the s-blade attachment and add in the pecan meal, grains of choice, olive oil (save 3 Tbsp.) and sea salt. Process until well combined. Add in the date paste 2 Tbsp. at a time and process until a dough ball forms. In a small bowl roll the coconut in the remaining olive oil. On a cutting board covered in saran wrap or other non-stick surface, spread out the coconut shreds. Remove the dough and scoop into 3 inch balls onto the coconut. Roll in the coconut and press into 3 inch flat dough shapes.

Line a dehydration tray with a mesh screen and place the breads directly on the screen. Place the trays in the dehydrator at 118 degrees for 4 hours. Check the breads and continue drying until firm yet still soft and moist.

Remove from the dehydrator and enjoy warm. Store the remainder in an airtight container in the refrigerator for up to 10 days.

"Native Fried" Bread

The Native American culture is credited with delicious flat crisp fried bread. This recipe is similar and a delicious bread to enjoy any time of the day, it also has 14 grams of protein per serving!

MAKES ROUGHLY 12 "NATIVE FRIED" BREADS

2 cup sprouted rye

½ cup walnut meal

½ cup soaked raisins

⅓ cup olive oil

¾ cup ground flax seeds

2 tsp. sea salt

Prepare the food processor for use with the s-blade attachment and add in the walnut meal, rye, olive oil (save 3 Tbsp.) and 1 tsp. sea salt. Process until well combined. Add in the soaked raisins 2 Tbsp. at a time and process until a dough ball forms. In a small bowl place the ground flax and remaining sea salt. On a cutting board covered in saran wrap or other non-stick surface spread out the flax seed. Remove the dough and scoop into 3 inch balls onto the flax seed. Roll in the flax seed and press into 3 inch flat dough shapes.

Line a dehydration tray with a mesh screen and place the breads directly on the screen. Place the trays in the dehydrator at 118 degrees for 4 hours. Check the breads and continue drying until firm yet still soft and moist.

Remove from the dehydrator and enjoy warm. Store the remainder in an airtight container in the refrigerator for up to 10 days.

Hawaiian Style Rolls

The islands are known for sweet breads with a multitude of influences. This bread makes use of some of the native island elements like macadamia nuts, raw honey, and coconut. This bread is a great source of essential fatty acids while also being a great side dish for any meal.

MAKES ROUGHLY 12 ROLLS

2   cups macadamia nuts

2   cups coconut flour

⅓   cup raw coconut oil or 4 Tbsp. coconut butter

⅓   cup raw honey

2   Tbsp. orange juice or zest

2   tsp. sea salt

Prepare the food processor for use with the s-blade attachment and add in the macadamia nuts, coconut oil or butter and raw honey. Process until well combined into almost a crème. Add in the coconut flour, orange and sea salt and pulse until a dough ball forms.

Line a dehydration tray with a mesh screen and place the dough in 3 inch balls directly on the screen. Place the trays in the dehydrator at 118 degrees for 4 hours. Check the breads and continue drying until firm yet still soft and moist.

Remove from the dehydrator and enjoy warm. Store the remainder in an airtight container in the refrigerator for up to 10 days.

Simple Dehydrated Pizza Crust

Pizza crusts are nice to have on an ongoing basis in your pantry or you can even prepare this dough and freeze it until ready for use.

MAKES ROUGHLY 6 PIZZA CRUSTS

6	cups sprouted buckwheat
2	cups ground golden flax seed
⅓	cup olive oil
4	Tbsp. dried Italian seasoning
2	cloves garlic
2	tsp. sea salt

Prepare the food processor for use with the s-blade attachment and add in all ingredients, but save the olive oil. Process the ingredients until well combined. Add in the olive oil from the top while on and process further until a dough ball forms.

Line a cutting board with saran wrap or your choice of non-stick surface. Divide the dough into 4-6 even segments and press out into a pizza crust shape. Then line 2 dehydration trays with mesh screens and place the dough directly on the screens. Place the trays in the dehydrator at 118 degrees for 4 hours. Check the crusts and continue drying until firm yet still soft and moist.

Remove from the dehydrator and enjoy warm. Store the remainder in an airtight container in the refrigerator for up to 10 days.

Marinated Nuts & Seeds

Nuts and seeds are a great source of essential minerals and healthy fats that stimulate the body nourishing its vital systems. Nuts and seeds provide a wealth of vitamins important for daily vibrant health as well. Enjoying dehydrated nuts and seeds provides a nutritious snack without sacrificing flavor or texture. Dehydrating your nuts and seeds according to this process will provide you and your family with crunchy tasty snacks that can be stored until ready to enjoy.

Follow these basic steps as they apply to the following recipes and you will find great success with these pantry staples.

For all nut and seed recipes:

1. Begin by properly soaking and sprouting the nuts and seeds according to the following chart:

Variety	Soak Time
Almonds	8 hours
Cashews	6 hours
Golden Flax Seeds	20 minutes
Macadamia Nuts	6 hours
Pecans	4 hours
Pistachios	4 hours
Pumpkin Seeds	4 hours
Seasame Seeds	20 minutes
Sunflower Seeds	4 hours
Walnuts	4 hours

2. Then rinse the nuts or seeds well and store in the refrigerator until you are ready to enjoy.

3. For all recipes be sure the nuts and seeds are completely done drying before storing in order to prevent molds or yeast from forming.

4. When you are shopping for nuts and seeds make sure they are raw and unpasteurized, to have great results in this chapter.

5. All recipes may be doubled or tripled depending on your needs, if looking to do even larger batches, be sure to do in separate containers for best results so the flavor of the marinade does not become overwhelming.

Spicy Almonds

Spicy almonds are a great pick me up and the smoky spicy flavor of these will leave you wanting more for sure! Enjoy as a garnish on a salad or by the handful.

MAKES ROUGHLY 3½ CUPS

4 cups raw almonds, soaked and sprouted

For the marinade:

½ cup coconut aminos (can also use Braggs, wheat free Tamari or Nama Shoyu)

¼ cup extra virgin olive oil

2 Tbsp. raw agave nectar

2 Tbsp. chili powder

1 tsp. cayenne pepper

1 tsp. lime juice

1 chipotle pepper

1 red bell pepper

1 tsp. sea salt

In a basic blender combine all marinade ingredients and blend until well combined. Then in a mid-sized mixing bowl toss together the nuts, after they have been well cleaned, and the marinade tossing until all nuts are well coated with marinade. Line a dehydration tray with a mesh screen and your choice of non-stick drying sheet and pour nuts over the sheet spreading them out evenly over the tray. They should form one layer across without being overlapped. Place the tray in the dehydrator at 118 degrees. Let dry for 4 hours then remove the non-stick sheet transferring the nuts directly to the screen. Let dry another 8 hours or until completely dry at 118 degrees. Store in an airtight container until ready to enjoy.

Fusion Nuts

One day while experimenting with a variety of leftovers in the kitchen, we discovered this delicious blend of flavors, and it has been a kitchen staple of ours ever since. Feel free to add to this in your own unique way, making use of items from your own garden and leftover nuts and seeds.

MAKES ROUGHLY 4 CUPS

4   cups mixed nuts, soaked and sprouted (we typically use almonds, macadamia nuts, and pistachios)

½   cup sesame seeds, soaked 20 minutes

For the marinade:

½   cup coconut aminos (can also use Braggs, wheat free Tamari or Nama Shoyu)

¼   cup extra virgin olive oil

3   Tbsp. raw honey or maple syrup

2   Tbsp. mild yellow curry powder

1   tsp. ground basil, or 2-3 leaves fresh basil

1   tsp. ground dried onion, or 2 fresh green onions

1   clove garlic

1   tsp. sea salt

In a basic blender combine all marinade ingredients and blend until well combined. Then in a mid-sized mixing bowl toss together the nuts, after they have been well cleaned, the sesame seeds and the marinade, tossing the mixture until well coated. Line a dehydration tray with a mesh screen and your choice of non-stick drying sheet and pour the mixture over the sheet spreading it out evenly to form one basic layer across the sheet. Place the tray in the dehydrator at 118 degrees. Let dry for 4 hours then remove the non-stick sheet transferring the nuts directly to the screen. Let dry another 8 hours or until completely dry at 118 degrees. Store in an airtight container until ready to enjoy.

Buttery Walnuts

These tasty walnuts were created the first Christmas that I was in the restaurant business. We were looking for something that would bring in some holiday cheer, warm the palette yet still provide a healthful snack during this festive time of the year. This is a fast and easy recipe with only a few ingredients. They look fantastic packaged in bags with ribbons for healthy delicious gifts to share with all of those on your holiday cheer list.

MAKES ROUGHLY 7 CUPS

8 cups raw walnuts, soaked 4 hours

For the marinade:

1 cup raw agave or raw honey

⅓ cup extra virgin olive oil

2 Tbsp. vanilla flavor or vanilla paste

1 Tbsp. sea salt, large flakes are fun to use in this recipe as well

1 tsp. ginger juice (optional)

Begin by whisking all marinade ingredients in a small bowl until well combined. Then in a mid-sized mixing bowl, toss together the nuts (after they have been soaked and well cleaned) and the marinade, tossing until all the nuts are well coated. Line a dehydration tray with a mesh screen and your choice of a non-stick drying sheet and pour the nuts over the sheet, spreading out evenly over 1-2 sheets so that the nuts do not overlap. Place the tray or trays in the dehydrator at 118 degrees. Let dry for 4 hours then remove the non-stick sheet transferring the nuts directly to the screen. Let dry another 8 hours or until completely dry at 118 degrees. Store in an airtight container until ready to enjoy.

Cinnamon Pecans

The aroma of these nuts floating through your house will surely attract attention! Cinnamon also serves as a great digestive aid, so these nuts are a go to item for a healthy dose of nutrition, providing your daily requirement of Vitamin E, A, and B1 as well as potassium, magnesium, calcium and protein.

MAKES ROUGHLY 7 CUPS

6   cups pecans, soaked 4 hours

For the marinade:

1   cup raw agave nectar or raw honey

¼   cup extra virgin olive oil

2   Tbsp. cinnamon

1   tsp. nutmeg

1   tsp. vanilla flavoring or vanilla paste

1   tsp. sea salt

Begin by whisking all marinade ingredients in a small bowl until well combined. Then in a mid-sized mixing bowl toss together the nuts, after they have been well cleaned, and the marinade tossing until all the nuts are well coated. Line a dehydration tray with mesh screen and your choice of non-stick drying sheet and pour nuts over the sheet spreading the nuts out evenly so that they form a single layer that does not overlap. Place the tray in the dehydrator at 118 degrees. Let dry for 4 hours then remove the non-stick sheet transferring the nuts directly to the screen. Let dry another 8 hours or until completely dry at 118 degrees. Store in an airtight container until ready to enjoy.

Rosemary Marcona Almonds

The Marcona almond, known as the "Queen of Almonds," is an almond varietal which originated in Spain. They are typically softer and flatter than other varieties and have an inherit round sweet flavor. As a result, we recommend soaking this variety for only 6 hours and then rinsing and letting sit 4 additional hours before use.

MAKES ROUGHLY 5 CUPS

6   cups raw Marcona almonds, soaked

For the marinade:

½   cup extra virgin olive oil
2   Tbsp. fresh rosemary
1   clove garlic
1   Tbsp. sea salt
2   drops essential rosemary oil

First dehydrate the raw soaked almonds for 2 hours to begin drying process. Then remove and place in mid-sized bowl. In a basic blender combine all marinade ingredient. Pour the marinade over the semi-dry almonds and toss well until all nuts are coated with the marinade. Let mixture sit for 1 hour for best results.

Line a dehydration tray with a mesh screen and your choice of a non-stick drying sheet and pour nuts over the sheet spreading the nuts out evenly over the sheet so that they create one even layer that does not overlap. Place the tray in the dehydrator at 118 degrees. Let dry for 4 hours then remove the non-stick sheet transferring the nuts directly to the screen. Let dry another 4 hours or until completely dry at 118 degrees. Store in an airtight container until ready to enjoy.

Hawaiian Macadamia Nuts

Whisk yourself away to the sweet aroma of the islands with this island inspired nut combination. Macadamia nuts are high in healthy essential monounsaturated oils, contributing to their status as a life-enhancing nut, providing not only longevity of life but also important proteins.

MAKES ROUGHLY 6 CUPS

- 6 cups raw macadamia nuts, soaked 6 hours
- ½ cup coconut flakes

For the marinade:

- 1 cup raw agave nectar or raw honey, or 2 oz. sugarcane juice
- ⅛ cup coconut oil
- 2 Tbsp. lime juice
- 1 tsp. vanilla flavoring or vanilla paste
- 1 tsp. sea salt

First blend all marinade ingredients in a basic blender until well combined. Then in a mid-sized mixing bowl toss together the nuts, after they have been well cleaned, and the coconut shreds. Add in the marinade and toss the entire mixture well until all contents are well coated. Let it sit for 20 minutes so the coconut may absorb more of the marinade.

Line a dehydration tray with a mesh screen and your choice of a non-stick drying sheet and pour nuts over the sheet, spreading the mixture out evenly so that it creates one even layer that does not overlap. Place the tray in the dehydrator at 118 degrees. Let dry for 4 hours then remove the non-stick sheet transferring the nuts directly to the screen. Let dry another 8 hours or until completely dry at 118 degrees. Store in an airtight container until ready to enjoy.

Living Trail Mix

Trail mix is a fun way to get a full spectrum of vitamins and minerals in your daily diet. It's also a great way to combine flavor and texture. Make this trail mix your own by combining your favorite nuts, seeds and fruits.

MAKES ROUGHLY 7 CUPS

6   cups raw nuts and seeds, soaked and sprouted (sunflower seeds, pumpkin seeds, almonds, and pistachios make a nice blend)

1   cup raw raisins, soaked

½   cup dried figs, diced and soaked

For the marinade:

1   red bell pepper or ½ cup coconut aminos, Braggs or Nama Shoyu

¼   cup extra virgin olive oil

2   Tbsp. raw agave or raw honey, or 2 drops Stevia

1   clove garlic

1   Tbsp. onion powder

1   Tbsp. garlic powder

1   Tbsp. dried parsley

1   Tbsp. spice blend of choice (could be Italian spices, Spanish spices or curry spices)

1   tsp. sea salt

First blend all marinade ingredients in a basic blender until well combined. Then in a mid-sized mixing bowl toss together the nuts, seed and the fruits after they have been well cleaned. Add in the marinade and toss well until all contents are evenly coated. Let it sit for 20 minutes so the mixture may absorb more of the marinade.

Line a dehydration tray with a mesh screen and your choice of a non-stick drying sheet and pour mixture over the sheet spreading out the mixture evenly so that it creates one layer that does not overlap. Place the tray in the dehydrator at 118 degrees. Let dry for 4 hours then remove the non-stick sheet transferring the nuts directly to the screen. Let dry another 8 hours or until completely dry at 118 degrees. Store in an airtight container until ready to enjoy.

Goji Nut Party

The wisdom of the ancients should not be overlooked; this blend of goji berries and nuts, provides an anti-aging opportunity not found in your basic blend of mixed nuts. It is well demonstrated by the Tibetan culture, who has used the goji berry for it's life enhancing qualities for centuries. This mixture contains 10 times the Vitamin C of an orange, powerful antioxidants, significant amounts of protein and dietary fiber.

MAKES ROUGHLY 6 CUPS

- 3   cups cashews or macadamia nuts, soaked
- 2   cups goji berries, soaked
- 1   cup dried mulberries, soaked (optional)
- 1   cup cacao nibs, soaked

For the marinade:

- ½   cup soak water from goji berries
- ¼   cup raw agave, raw honey or 2 drops Stevia
- ¼   cup of the soaked goji berries
- 2   Tbsp. coconut oil
- 1   tsp. vanilla flavoring or vanilla paste
- 1   tsp. sea salt

First blend all marinade ingredients in a basic blender until well combined. Then in a mid-sized mixing bowl toss together the nuts, cacao nibs, and fruits after they have been well cleaned. Add in the marinade, tossing until the entire mixture is well coated.

Line a dehydration tray with a mesh screen and your choice of non-stick drying sheet and pour mixture over the sheet. Place the tray in the dehydrator at 118 degrees. Let dry for 4 hours then remove the non-stick sheet transferring the nuts directly to the screen. Let dry another 8 hours or until completely dry at 118 degrees. Store in an airtight container until ready to enjoy.

Spicy Seed Mix

Spicy seeds are a great ball-game companion and fantastic as a garnish on tacos, tostadas, and in taco salad. This mixture also contains a significant amount of chlorophyll along with the protein, which makes it a great way to add additional protein to your living foods dishes.

MAKES ROUGHLY 6 CUPS

2   cups pumpkin seeds, soaked
    and sprouted
2   cups sunflower seeds, soaked
    and sprouted
1   cup sesame seeds, soaked
    20 minutes
1   cup golden flax seeds, soaked
    20 minutes

For the marinade:

1   Roma tomato *
1   red bell pepper *
⅛   cup extra virgin olive oil
1   clove garlic
2   Tbsp. raw agave or raw honey
2   Tbsp. lime juice or lemon juice
2   Tbsp. chili powder
1   tsp. cayenne pepper
1   tsp. sea salt

First toss together the seeds to create a basic seed mixture in a mid-sized mixing bowl and let sit while completing the marinade, the flax seeds will be sticky and this is okay. Then blend all marinade ingredients in a basic blender until well combined. Pour the marinade over the seed mixture and toss well until all seeds are well coated.

Line a dehydration tray with a mesh screen and your choice of non-stick drying sheet and pour the mixture over the sheet spreading the mixture out evenly over the tray to create a single layer that does not overlap. Place the tray in the dehydrator at 118 degrees. Let dry for 4 hours then remove the non-stick sheet transferring the nuts directly to the screen. Let dry another 4 hours or until completely dry at 118 degrees. Store in an airtight container until ready to enjoy.

*You may substitute ½ cup Braggs or coconut aminos for these two ingredients if you'd like, this will create a stronger flavor.

Tutti Frutti

Fruits help to balance nuts in nut and seed blends by providing additional sources of nutrition and minimizing the amount of raw oils in the blend. This is a very special mixture as it is designed to be completely balanced providing your daily source of Vitamins A, C, E, essential fatty acids, magnesium, potassium and calcium, as well as a significant source of protein, over 8 grams per serving.*

MAKES ROUGHLY 6 CUPS

- **2 cups raw walnuts, soaked and sprouted**
- **1 cup raw pecans, soaked and sprouted**
- **1 cup raw almonds, soaked and sprouted**
- **¾ cup hemp seeds**
- **½ cup figs, diced and soaked**
- **¼ cup goji berries, soaked**
- **1 cup fresh apples, diced**
- **¼ cup dried apricots, soaked**
- **2 Tbsp. orange zest**

For the marinade:

- **½ cup raw agave nectar, raw honey or maple syrup**
- **⅛ cup coconut oil**
- **2 Tbsp. orange juice**
- **1 tsp. vanilla flavoring or vanilla paste**
- **1 tsp. sea salt**

Begin by placing all Tutti Frutti mix ingredients in large sized mixing bowl and tossing together. Then blend all marinade ingredients in a basic blender until well combined. Pour the marinade over the nuts, seeds and fruit. Let it sit for 20 minutes so the mixture may absorb more of the marinade.

Line two dehydration trays with a mesh screen and your choice of non-stick drying sheets and pour mixture over the sheets spreading them out evenly to create a single layer that does not overlap. Place the trays in the dehydrator at 118 degrees. Let dry for 4 hours then remove the trays transferring the nuts directly to the screen. Let dry another 8 hours or until completely dry at 118 degrees. Store in an airtight container until ready to enjoy.

*Serving size ½ cup.

Dessert Date Blend

Dessert can be as simple as this sweet blend of dates and nuts over some fresh fruit. These also make a high protein breakfast snack and are delicious over oatmeal. Dates provide a significant source of potassium as well as B vitamins, so they are regarded as a beneficial energy boosting treat.

MAKES ROUGHLY 4 CUPS

4   cups raw almonds or
     pistachios, soaked and
     sprouted
1   cup dates, diced and pitted
     soaked 25 minutes

For the marinade:

4   dates
1   cup water or coconut water
⅛   cup coconut oil or extra virgin
     olive oil
1   tsp. cinnamon
1   tsp. vanilla flavoring or vanilla
     paste (optional)
1   tsp. sea salt

First blend all marinade ingredients in a basic blender until well combined. Then in a mid-sized mixing bowl toss together the nuts, after they have been well cleaned, and the marinade tossing well until all nuts are well coated.

Line a dehydration tray with your choice of non-stick drying sheet and pour nut mixture over the sheet spreading out the mixture evenly over the tray to form a single layer that does not overlap. Place the tray in the dehydrator at 118 degrees. Let dry for 4 hours then remove the non-stick sheet transferring the nuts directly to the screen. Let dry another 6 hours or until completely dry at 118 degrees. Store in an airtight container until ready to enjoy.

Wraps

Tacos, burritos, tortellini and more can all be made using the Sedona as your basic tool to create mouthwatering wraps. Simple wraps are one of the key benefits of owning a dehydrator. Making your own fresh wraps is easy and a great way to prepare for a weeks worth of delicious cuisine. The wraps in this book can all be prepared in advance and stored in the refrigerator in an airtight container for easy use.

Remember that wraps should be soft and flexible when done and as a result, they are probably one of the more delicate dehydrating techniques to begin with. It's easy to soften most wraps by placing them under a damp clean towel if they get a little crisp around the edges. Except where instructed, we don't recommend flipping your wraps during the drying process as they will shrink and the edges will curl.

Simple Seed Wraps

The simple seed wrap is created using vegetable fiber and seeds. The more seeds you use the denser the wrap will be. By combining a few types of seeds, you will enhance the nutritional benefit of the wrap. Be careful not to overdo it though to avoid a bitter tasting wrap. Here is a suggested guideline:

2   **cups ground flax seeds**

½   **cup sprouted quinoa**

4   **Tbsp. ground chia seed or hemp seed**

1   **cup yellow squash or zucchini**

3   **cups water**

2   **Tbsp. seasoning of choice (I love a basic Italian spice here)**

1   **tsp. sea salt**

Begin by first filling the blender with water, seasoning and squash. Blend these into a basic purée. Then add in all seeds and blend again. Blend until a thick paste is formed. Since you are using flax the mixture will naturally thicken as it sits so you will want to spread the wraps out over the dehydration trays pretty quickly.

Line 3 dehydration trays with a non-stick drying sheet of your choice. Then evenly spread mixture out over the trays evenly to create a thin layer about ⅛ inch thick. You should have a nice layer that you cannot see through on each tray.

Place dehydration trays in the dehydrator at 118 degrees for 4-6 hours until wrap is completely dry to the touch. Flip the non-stick drying sheet over and carefully pull back the wrap. Cut the wrap down into the portion sizes you will use to create your final dishes and store indefinitely in the refrigerator in an airtight container.

Vegetable Wraps

This wrap makes use of basic juicing leftovers and can be easier to digest than heavier wraps. It also has a very distinct flavor that compliments several other fresh fruits, in particular avocado!!

2   cups ground flax seeds

2   cups juice pulp (I love carrot, beet, and celery)

1   cup yellow squash or zucchini

4   cups water

1   red bell pepper or tomato

1   tsp. sea salt

Begin by first filling the blender with water, pulp and squash. Blend these into a basic purée. Then add in all seeds and blend again. Blend until a thick paste is formed. Since you are using flax the mixture will naturally thicken as it sits so you will want to spread the wraps out over the dehydration trays pretty quickly.

Line 3 dehydration trays with a screen and a non-stick drying sheet of choice. Then evenly spread mixture out over the trays evenly to create a thin layer about ⅛ inch thick over the screens. You should have a nice layer that you cannot see through on each tray.

Place dehydration sheets in the dehydrator at 118 degrees for 4-6 hours until wrap is completely dry to the touch. Flip the non-stick drying sheet over and carefully pull back the wrap. Cut the wrap down into the portion sizes you will use to create your final dishes and store indefinitely in the refrigerator in an airtight container.

Curry Wraps

Curry can be mild or spicy depending on your preference. I love a mild yellow curry for this wrap and it pairs perfectly with hummus and tahini.

2   cups ground flax seeds

1   cup yellow squash

4   Tbsp. ground chia seed

2½ cups water

2   Tbsp. ground dried curry powder

1   tsp. sea salt

Begin by first filling the blender with water, seasoning, and squash. Blend these into a basic purée. Then add in all seeds and blend again. Blend until a thick paste is formed. Since you are using flax the mixture will naturally thicken as it sits so you will want to spread the wraps out over the dehydration trays pretty quickly.

Line 2 dehydration trays with a mesh screen and a non-stick drying sheet of choice. Then evenly spread mixture out over the trays evenly to create a thin layer about ⅛ inch thick. You should have a nice layer that you cannot see through on each tray.

Place dehydration sheets in the dehydrator at 118 degrees for 4-6 hours until wrap is completely dry to the touch. Flip the non-stick drying sheet over and carefully pull back the wrap. Cut the wrap down into the portion sizes you will use to create your final dishes and store indefinitely in the refrigerator in an airtight container.

Sushi Wraps

Sushi is fun and delightful treat all year round. Sea vegetables are high in essential B vitamins and iron. This wrap makes use of the benefit of sea vegetables but gives you a stronger wrap than a sheet of nori can provide. Allowing you to make sushi that can sit and hold up as you entertain and makes a great conversation piece.

1	**cup ground dark flax seeds**
1	**cup dulse or laver**
1	**cup coconut flesh**
2	**cups water**
⅛	**cup sesame seeds (garnish)**

Begin by first filling the blender with water, sea vegetables and cleaned coconut flesh. Blend these into a basic purée until a thick paste is formed. Since you are using flax the mixture will naturally thicken as it sits so you will want to spread the wraps out over the dehydration trays pretty quickly.

Line 2 dehydration trays with a mesh screen and a non-stick drying sheet of choice. Then evenly spread mixture out over the trays evenly to create a thin layer about ⅛ inch thick. You should have a nice layer that you cannot see through on each tray. Sprinkle the sesame seeds evenly over the top of each.

Place dehydration sheets in the dehydrator at 118 degrees for 4-6 hours until wrap is completely dry to the touch. Flip the non-stick drying sheet over and carefully pull back the wrap. Cut the wrap down into the portion sizes you will use to create your final dishes and store indefinitely in the refrigerator in an airtight container.

Simple Tortillas

Simple tortillas can be made into round shapes or created as a tray and cut down to size. These are an important pantry staple for really transitioning to the living foods lifestyle. There are a few options for you with this recipe, enjoy both and find your own favorite combination!

2	cups sprouted buckwheat or corn
1	cup ground flax seeds
2	cups fresh water
2	Tbsp. chili powder
1	tsp. garlic powder
1	tsp. sea salt

Begin by first filling the blender with water, seasoning and sprouted buckwheat or corn. Blend these into a basic purée. Then add in all seeds and blend until a thick paste is formed. Since you are using flax the mixture will naturally thicken as it sits so you will want to spread the wraps out over the dehydration trays pretty quickly.

Line 3 dehydration trays with a mesh screen and a non-stick drying sheet of choice. Then evenly spread mixture out over the trays evenly to create a thin layer about ⅛ inch thick. You should have a nice layer that you cannot see through on each tray. Or create 4-6 inch rounds on the lined dehydration trays, this may take more trays but it's fun to have these round tortillas, especially for kids!

Place dehydration trays in the dehydrator at 118 degrees for 4-6 hours until wrap is completely dry to the touch. Flip the non-stick drying sheet over and carefully pull back the wrap. Cut the wrap down into the portion sizes you will use to create your final dishes and store indefinitely in the refrigerator in an airtight container.

Strawberry Wraps

Strawberry crêpes, fruit roll ups and more can be made with these delicious wraps. As these wraps are mostly fruit based, you can also cut them down into strips as fruit leathers!

6	**cups fresh strawberries**
4	**Tbsp. raw agave nectar**
½	**cup golden flax seeds or**
	4 Tbsp. psyllium husk
1	**cup raw coconut flesh, cleaned**

Begin by first filling the blender with strawberries, agave, and coconut. Blend these into a basic purée. Then add in seeds or psyllium and blend again until a thick paste is formed.

Line 2 dehydration trays with a mesh screen and a non-stick drying sheet of choice. Then evenly spread mixture out over the trays evenly to create a thin layer about ⅛ inch thick. You should have a nice layer that you cannot see through on each tray.

Place dehydration trays in the dehydrator at 118 degrees for 4-6 hours until wrap is completely dry to the touch. Flip the non-stick drying sheet over and carefully pull back the wrap. Cut the wrap down into the portion sizes you will use to create your final dishes and store indefinitely in the refrigerator in an airtight container.

Caramel Wraps

Caramel wraps are great for desserts and breakfast! These are versatile and delicious...

2   cups young Thai coconut flesh
1   cup young Thai coconut water
2/3 cup ground flax seeds
4   Tbsp. raw agave nectar
1   Tbsp. cinnamon
1   Tbsp. pumpkin pie spice
1   Tbsp. maca root
1   tsp. sea salt

Begin by first filling the blender with coconut flesh and water, seasoning, and agave. Blend these into a basic purée. Then add in flax seeds and blend again. Blend until a thick paste is formed.

Line 2 dehydration trays with a mesh screen and a non-stick drying sheet of choice. Then evenly spread mixture out over the trays evenly to create a thin layer about ⅛ inch thick. You should have a nice layer that you cannot see through on each tray.

Place dehydration trays in the dehydrator at 118 degrees for 4-6 hours until wrap is completely dry to the touch. Flip the non-stick drying sheet over and carefully pull back the wrap. Cut the wrap down into the portion sizes you will use to create your final dishes and store indefinitely in the refrigerator in an airtight container.

Chili Wraps

Chili wraps really are the spice in any given recipe, these are a bit thicker and create a great base for things like empanadas!

½   cup sprouted buckwheat
⅔   cup butternut squash
½   cup yellow corn
1   cup ground golden flax seed
2   cups water
4   Tbsp. extra virgin olive oil
1   Tbsp. chili powder
1   tsp. cayenne pepper
1   tsp. sea salt

Begin by first filling the blender with water, buckwheat, corn seasoning and squash. Blend these into a basic purée. Then add in flax seeds and blend again. Blend until a thick paste is formed.

Line 3 dehydration trays with a mesh screen and a non-stick drying sheet of choice. Then evenly spread mixture out over the trays evenly to create a thin layer about ¼ inch thick. You should have a nice layer that you cannot see through on each tray, or create individual rounds on each dehydration tray. This may take more trays to accomplish but the wraps will then be perfect for filling.

Place dehydration trays in the dehydrator at 118 degrees for 4-6 hours until wrap is completely dry to the touch. Flip the non-stick drying sheet over and carefully pull back the wrap. Cut the wrap down into the portion sizes you will use to create your final dishes and store indefinitely in the refrigerator in an airtight container.

Greens Wraps

When going green there are many ways to accomplish getting this dense nutrition in your diet while still enjoying a culinary treat. This wrap is fun to incorporate into your daily diet as it is well balanced and naturally a bit sweet!

2   cups young Thai coconut flesh or 2 cups green vegetable pulp from the juicer

1   cup ground golden flax seeds

1   cup fresh water

4   Tbsp. extra virgin olive oil

2   Tbsp. spirulina

2   Tbsp. dulse flakes

2   Tbsp. agave nectar

1   tsp. sea salt

Begin by first filling the blender with water, pulp or coconut, seasoning, and agave. Blend these into a basic purée. Then add in all seeds and blend again. Blend until a thick paste is formed. Since you are using flax the mixture will naturally thicken as it sits so you will want to spread the wraps out over the dehydration trays pretty quickly.

Line 3 dehydration trays with a mesh screen and a non-stick drying sheet of choice. Then evenly spread mixture out over the trays evenly to create a thin layer about ⅛ inch thick. You should have a nice layer that you cannot see through on each tray.

Place dehydration trays in the dehydrator at 118 degrees for 4-6 hours until wrap is completely dry to the touch. Flip the non-stick drying sheet over and carefully pull back the wrap. Cut the wrap down into the portion sizes you will use to create your final dishes and store indefinitely in the refrigerator in an airtight container.

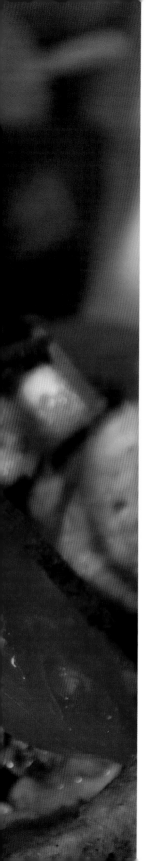

Garnishes

Garnishes are simple pantry basics that can spice up dishes, provide a finishing touch on any entrée or dress up a dish for entertaining. These garnishes make use of other fresh recipes and are a great example of how you can really work with your Sedona dehydrator to eliminate waste in your living foods kitchen.

Everyday Cheese

Everyday cheese is a natural by product of the alfredo sauce in this book, or other similar recipes you may have in your kitchen. The idea behind everyday cheese is to use it as a spice or a topping on fresh salads. It adds the nutritional benefit of B12 and a hint of flavor that can keep you living foods diet exciting and new.

MAKES 1 TRAY

2　cups of Alfredo Sauce (see recipe below.)

4　Tbsp. nutritional yeast or dulse flakes

4　sun-dried tomatos

1　tsp. sea salt

Juice of 1 lemon

For Alfredo Sauce:

MAKES 3 CUPS OF ALFREDO SAUCE

2　cups macadamia nuts or cashew

½　cup lemon juice

4　Tbsp. raw agave, honey or 2 drops liquid Stevia

1　Roma tomato

1　tsp. sea salt

¾　cup water

In a basic blender simply add all ingredients and blend to a thick paste. Then line a dehydration tray with a mesh screen and your choice of non-stick drying sheet. Gently spread on contents of blender onto the dehydration sheet no thicker than ⅓ of an inch.

Place the dehydration tray into the dehydrator at 118 degrees for 12 hours or until completely dry. Crumble the cheese and store in an airtight container. If dried all the way, this topping does not need to be refrigerated. You may decide to remove the cheese shortly before so it still contains moisture. At this point the cheese can be cut down into pieces and served on a cheese tray.

For Alfredo Sauce: Blend the nuts, lemon juice and ¾ cup water until a thick puree forms. Add the remaining ingredients and puree until well combined.

Sedona Dried Tomato

Dried tomatoes are a delicious pantry option because they fit so well on so many dishes. Use this recipe to create a great garnish!

MAKES 2-3 CUPS

4   Roma tomato, diced

1   red bell pepper

4   Tbsp. extra virgin olive oil

1   tsp. raw agave nectar

1   clove garlic

4   leaves fresh basil

1   tsp. sea salt

In a personal blender blend everything, but save the tomatoes. In a mid-sized mixing bowl toss the tomato and the fresh blend. Toss together the tomato and the blended mixture.

Line a dehydration tray with mesh screen and your choice of non-stick drying sheet. Remove entire mixture and spread out evenly over the tray. Then place the dehydration tray in the dehydrator at 125 degrees for the first 2 hours. Remove the tray and toss the mixture, and then transfer onto the mesh screen covering the tray. Dehydrate at 118 degrees for the next 4-6 hours until completely dry. Remove from dehydrator and store in an airtight storage container indefinitely.

Firecracker Crisps

Firecracker crisps are a great use of leftover wrap pieces, but they are especially good with the basic seed wrap. These were inspired by one of our extended family members at 118, Jose, who always comes up with great and delicious Spanish influenced recipes. He likes to make them hot, I prefer them on the milder side, but either way they are a really fun garnish to have for any dish.

MAKES 6 CUPS

8   cups left over wrap pieces

4   Tbsp. olive oil

2   Tbsp. chili powder

1   tsp. cayenne pepper

1   Tbsp. sea salt

1   tsp. agave nectar

Begin by laying our wrap pieces and slicing them lengthwise into pieces about ½ inch in thickness and 2-3 inches long. In a mid–sized mixing bowl toss together all ingredients until wrap is well coated with seasoning.

Line a dehydration tray with a mesh screen and place the crisps directly on the screen so they criss cross if desired. Place the dehydration tray in the dehydrator at 118 degrees for 8-12 hours. Remove when completely dry. Transfer crisps to an airtight container for storage indefinitely.

Simply Dehydrated 118 Spice Blend

Spices are a great way to add flavor to dishes and many fresh herbs also have medicinal benefits, leading to a healthy and functional way to create your next dish. This is a basic spice blend that we create at 118 degrees for several of our dishes!

MAKES ROUGHLY ½ CUP

- **4   cloves garlic, thinly sliced**
- **1   cup onion pieces, sliced thin**
- **4   cups fresh basil**
- **1   red bell pepper, sliced thin (optional)**
- **1   cup fresh rosemary**

Line 2 dehydration trays with mesh screens. Lay out all ingredients so they cover the trays. Then place the dehydration trays in the dehydrator at 118 degrees. Dry for 12 hours until all components are completely dry.

Remove the trays and combine all dried items in a mid-sized bowl. Toss together, breaking large pieces into smaller pieces. Place 1 cup of dried items in the personal blender or in a spice grinder and grind down. Once mixture is well ground place in an airtight storage container for indefinitely storage.

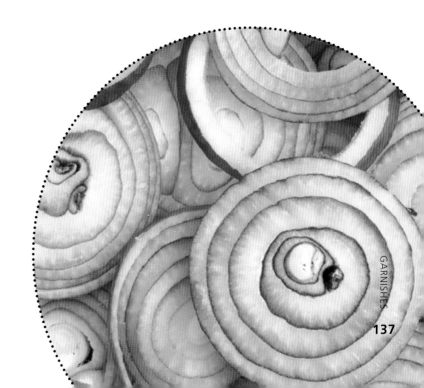

GARNISHES

Super Food Sprinkle

Super foods are a great way to add additional functional health benefits to foods of all types from appetizers to salads. This can be altered based on what you have laying around in your kitchen.

MAKES ROUGHLY 2 CUPS

2   cups kale leaves

1   cup sprouted red quinoa

1   cup golden flax seed or ½ cup sprouted hemp seeds

2   Tbsp. nutritional yeast or 2 Tbsp. dulse flakes (or both!)

2   Tbsp. coconut oil, hemp oil or flax oil

2   Tbsp. spirulina, chlorella or other basic greens blend

1   Tbsp. chili powder

1   Tbsp. kelp granules

4   fresh garlic cloves

1   wedge of lemon

In a basic food processor with the s-blade attachment in place, pulse all ingredients, but save the lemon. Pulse until a basic chopped combination is achieved. Transfer mixture to a mid-sized mixing bowl and squeeze lemon wedge over the top and massage gently into mixture.

Line a dehydration tray with a mesh screen and your choice of non-stick drying sheet. Transfer mixture onto the dehydration tray and evenly disperse over the tray. Place tray in the dehydrator at 118 degrees for 8-12 hours until the mixture is crisp and dry. Further pulse down if you choose to. This is an easy to use mixture that can be sprinkled over salads, sandwiches and more! Store in an airtight container indefinitely.

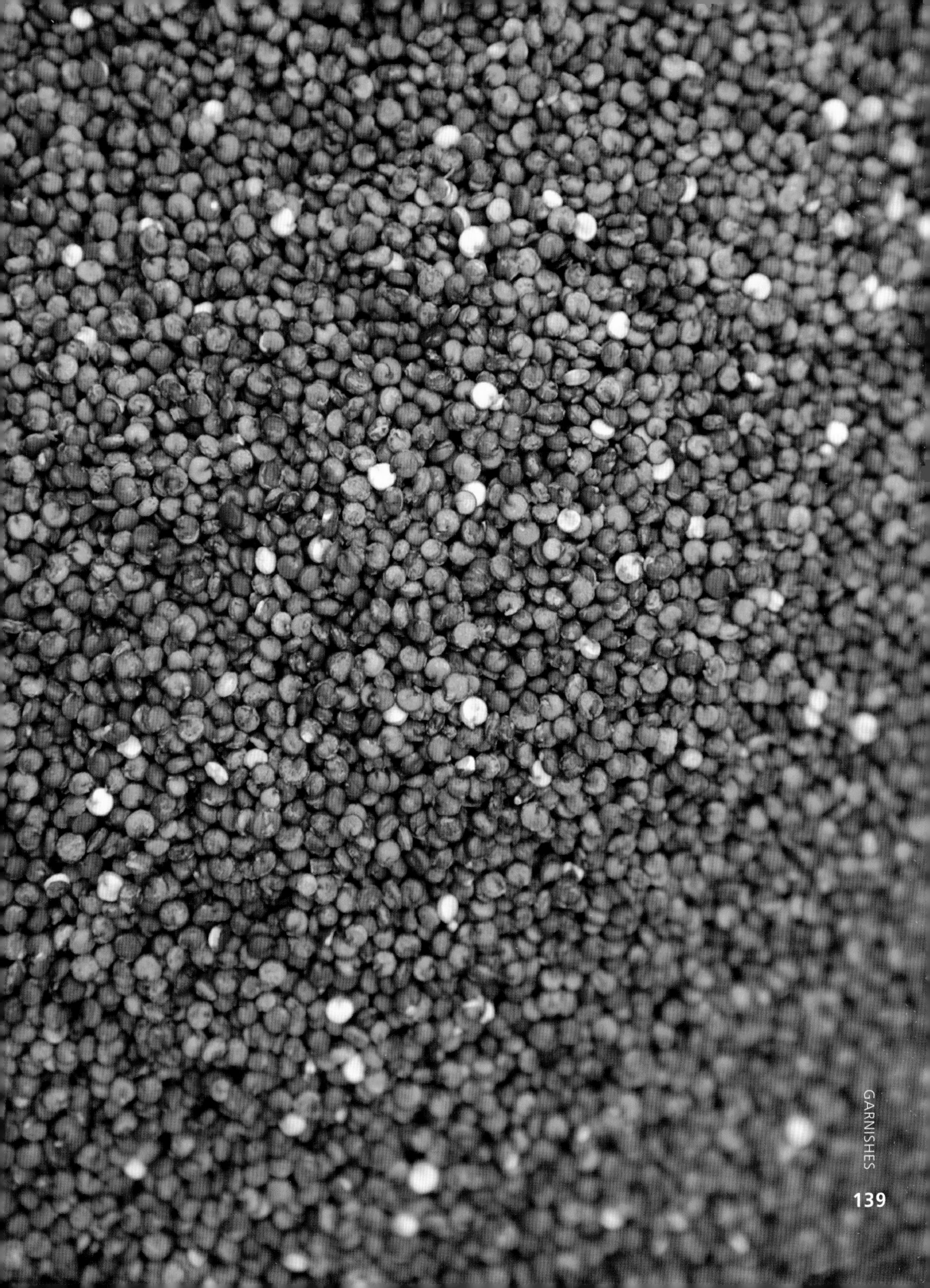

Pumpkin Seed Falafel

Pumpkin seed falafels are easy to make and save, providing a nutritional filling for a variety of wraps, hand-held options, and rice bowls. Pumpkin seeds are a good source of magnesium and also create a rich, decadent flavor.

MAKES ROUGHLY 16 FALAFELS

4   **cups sprouted pumpkin seeds**

2   **cups spinach**

1   **Roma tomato**

2   **cloves garlic**

½   **cup lemon juice**

1   **Tbsp. sea salt**

In a basic food processor with the s-blade attachment in place begin by combining all ingredients, but save the pumpkin seeds, and pulse until well combined. Put this mixture into a mid-sized bowl. Now add the pumpkin seeds to the food processor and process to a thick paste. Add in the first mixture and run until well combined.

Line a dehydration tray with mesh screens and your choice of non-stick sheet. Remove the falafel mixture from the food processor and place in a mid-sized mixing bowl. Scoop out the mixture 2 Tbsp. at a time onto the non-stick surface in falafel shapes. Make sure they do not touch but are close together. Scoop out the entire mixture onto the tray in the selected shape.

Place the falafel in the dehydrator at 125 degrees for 2 hours. Then remove non-stick drying sheet and transfer the falafel straight onto the mesh screen lining the tray. Place back in the dehydrator and dehydrate at 118 degrees for an additional 4-6 hours until firm but not hard. Remove from dehydrator and place in an airtight container in the refrigerator for 10-14 days.

Quinoa Croquettes

Quinoa is a great source of protein that is gluten-free, easy to absorb and a great resource for your fresh pantry.

MAKES ROUGHLY 12 CROQUETTES

- 4 cups sprouted red quinoa
- 1 cup macadamia nuts, cashews or pine nuts
- ½ cup fresh water or coconut water
- 2 cloves garlic
- 2 cups carrot pulp or 2 zucchini, diced
- 2 Tbsp. dried dill
- 2 Tbsp. onion powder
- 2 Tbsp. kelp granules
- 2 Tbsp. extra virgin olive oil
- 1 Tbsp. sea salt

In a basic blender combine all ingredients, but save the quinoa, blend to a thick paste. Transfer blend mix to a mid-sized mixing bowl and add in quinoa. Stir together until a thick paste is achieved.

Line two dehydration trays with mesh screens and your choice of non-stick drying sheets. Scoop mixture by the tablespoon into 3 Tbsp. croquettes 2 inches wide and 1 inch high.

Place in dehydrator at 125 degrees for 2 hours. Remove the croquettes and transfer them straight onto the mesh screen and place them back in the dehydrator. Dehydrate at 118 degrees for an additional 4-6 hours until dry but not hard. Remove the croquettes and store in the refrigerator for up to 14 days in an airtight container.

Walnut Filling

Walnut filling is perfect for tacos, enchiladas, hand-held lettuce cups and more. Enjoy alone with some fresh greens for a flavorful salad as well.

MAKES 3 CUPS

4 cups walnuts, soaked
½ cup chopped green onions
2 cloves garlic
4 sun-dried tomato, soaked
2 Tbsp. oregano
2 Tbsp. dulse flakes
2 Tbsp. chili powder
1 Tbsp. sea salt
1 tsp. onion powder

In a basic food processor with the s-blade attached, combine all ingredients and pulse until well combined but still holding body.

Line a dehydration tray with a mesh screen and your choice of non-stick drying sheet. Transfer the mixture to the dehydration tray and evenly disperse over drying sheet. Place the tray in the dehydrator at 118 degrees for 12 hours. To shorten drying time remove at 4 hours, toss and place directly on the screen.

Remove when soft and crunchy. Store in an airtight container in the refrigerator for up to 21 days.

Appetizers

Appetizers are a quick and easy way to introduce friends and family to the magic of the Sedona Dehydrator. The Sedona makes entertaining a cinch as many of these recipes can be placed in the dehydrator and taken out right before a delicious gathering among friends and family. These small dishes are also great accompaniments to salads and make a great first course for any meal.

Apple Walnut Stuffing

This stuffing, a seasonal favorite in our family, is delicious and easy to enjoy- serve it on top of an apple slice as an easy tapas plate at your next holiday gathering or as a side dish along one of the delicious entrées in this book.

MAKES 4 CUPS

4   cups walnuts, soaked

4   organic Fuji or Gala apples, diced

2   cups celery, diced

½   cup white onion, finely chopped

2   Tbsp. dried Italian seasoning

½   cup apple juice

4   Tbsp. extra virgin olive oil

1   clove garlic

1   Tbsp. sea salt

In a basic food processor with the s-blade attachment in place, process the nuts until well broken down. Then add in all remaining ingredients and pulse until well combined, yet still full of body.

Line 2 dehydration trays with mesh screens and non-stick drying sheets. Remove the stuffing and cover both sheets evenly dispersing the mixture. Place in the dehydrator at 118 degrees for 6 hours. About half way through the drying time toss to keep the mixture moist and move drying edges.

Remove and enjoy warm. Refrigerate leftovers in air-tight glass storage container for use within 3-5 days.

Butternut Soufflé

One word describes this dish- DELICIOUS! Soft and creamy on top with a firm crust this soufflé is a fun option to present and makes enjoying butternut squash a memorable experience.

MAKES 10 SOUFFLÉS

- 4 cups Basic Savory Crust (pg. 203)

- 4 cups butternut squash, cubed
- 1 cup water
- 4 Tbsp. psyllium husk or 6 Tbsp. ground golden flax seed
- ⅓ cup extra virgin olive oil
- 3 Tbsp. raw agave nectar
- 1 Tbsp. dried Italian seasoning
- 1 tsp. chili powder
- 2 cloves garlic
- 1 Tbsp. sea salt

Begin by blending butternut squash and water until a thick purée is formed. Add in all remaining ingredients and blend well. Once well combined to a light and fluffy consistency remove the mixture and place in mid-sized mixing bowl.

Line two dehydration trays with mesh screens and non-stick drying sheets. Then begin creating 3 inch rounds with the Basic Savory Crust mixture. Top each round with 4 oz. of soufflé mixture (this should be about 2 inches high). Place in the dehydrator at 118 degrees for 2-4 hours. Serve warm. Place leftover pieces in an airtight container in the refrigerator and enjoy within 3 days.

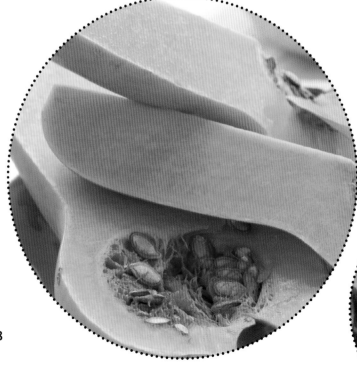

Cranberry Artichoke Torte

Create this dish any time of the year for a festive gathering full of color! These tortes are easy to prepare, artful and taste divine. One great thing about this recipe is you can easily modify the toppings to create culinary magic fresh from your garden or using left overs from your food pantry.

MAKES 8-12 TORTES

4 cups Basic Savory Crust (pg. 203)

2 cups fresh or frozen cranberries (thawed)

2 cups artichoke hearts (fresh or frozen)

⅓ cup agave nectar

⅓ cup extra virgin olive oil

4 Tbsp. dried Italian seasoning

2 cloves garlic

1 tsp. sea salt

Begin by using a basic food processor with the s-blade attachment and pulse the cranberries and artichoke hearts until well combined. Then add the remaining agave, oil, and seasoning and process for about 20 seconds.

Line a dehydration tray with a mesh screen and your choice of non-stick drying sheet. Press the torte crust into lined torte molds and invert onto sheet, or simply create 2 by 3 inch squares of crust ⅓ inch thick. Line each crust with another ½ inch of torte topping. Place in the dehydrator at 118 degrees for 4-6 hours until mostly dry but still a little bit moist to the touch. Serve fresh out of the dehydrator, on a party tray or individually. Store left overs in an airtight container for up to 3 days.

CA Fusion Roll

CA offers many fresh produce options year round, but CA also has a culinary collaboration of flavor, heavily influenced by the entire globe. This dish makes use of a variety of fresh flavor and is a great way to start any meal.

MAKES 4 SERVINGS

4   quarters of Curry Wraps tray
    (1 full tray cut into 4 even
    pieces- pg. 121)

For the sauce:

1   red bell pepper
4   Tbsp. extra virgin olive oil
1   green onion, bottom only
1   clove garlic
1   tsp. sea salt

For the filling:

1   hot house cucumber
1   Hass avocado, cut lengthwise
1   cup arugula or spinach
2   cups shredded carrots
4   green onions, green stalk only

Begin by placing each wrap on a cutting board. Line the bottom 2 inches of each wrap with filling ingredients, evenly dispersing over each wrap. Roll each wrap tightly and cut down into 1 inch pieces. Place the pieces next to each other standing up on a plate and garnish with sauce over the top or on the side.

Sushi 3 Ways

Simply dehydrated has a recipe for the best sushi wraps on the planet! Here are 3 creative ways to use them.

MAKES 4 APPETIZER PORTIONS

Mango Coconut Sushi

2 fresh mangos, cut thin
2 cups fresh coconut flesh
1 red bell pepper, cleaned and cut lengthwise
1 green onion
1 cup sushi rice (see recipe to the right)

Avocado Sushi

1 cup fresh shiitake mushrooms, cut lengthwise
2 cups avocado, diced
1 package enoki mushrooms
1 cup chopped chard
1 Tbsp. extra virgin olive oil or sesame oil
1 cup sushi rice (see recipe to the right)
Juice of 1 lemon*

Exotica Sushi

2 cups hot house cucumber, julienned
2 cups salad savoy, arugula or dandelion greens
8 slices pickled carrots
1 green onion
1 cup sushi rice (see recipe to the right)
2 oz. ginger juice *
1 Tbsp. agave nectar*

For each 4 segments of sushi wrap (1 whole tray, cut down into 4- pg. 122)

For sushi rice: 2 cups pine nuts or soaked cashews, 1 Tbsp. coconut butter or cashew butter, 1 tsp. sea salt, 1 cup cauliflower or jicama. In a food processor with the s-blade in place pulse all ingredients until well combined and holding together.
*Ingredients marked with a star should be hand tossed into the rice mixture before using.

Begin by lining wrap out flat on a cutting board. For each roll layer ingredients one on top of the other, beginning with rice mixture and then roll the wrap tightly around the ingredients forming a tight roll. Cut each roll into 4-6 slices and line up next to each other on a flat plate. Serve with your choice of Nama Shoyu, Tamari or coconut aminos.

Firecracker Rolls

These rolls are festive, sweet and spicy. Use this as en eye-catching centerpiece on your table or use it to brighten up a basic side salad.

MAKES 4 SERVINGS

4   pieces Simple Seed Wrap
    (pg. 116) or Vegetable Wraps
    (pg. 118)

For the sauce:

2   avocado
½   cup water
1   Tbsp. agave
1   tsp. sea salt
Juice of 1 lemon

For the filling:

1   cup of shredded green papaya
1   cup of shredded carrots
2   cups of spicy pepper slices (use
    hatch, Serrano, Thai peppers or
    jalapeños)
1   mango, cored and sliced
    lengthwise
1   red bell pepper, cored,
    cleaned, and sliced lengthwise

Prepare all vegetables, then in a personal blender combine all sauce ingredients and blend well. Follow this by lining up wraps on a cutting board, gently coat each wrap with 2 Tbsp. of the sauce and spread evenly over the bottom $^2/_3$ of each wrap. Fill each wrap evenly with ¼ of vegetable pieces, lining them up lengthwise. Roll the wrap tightly around the vegetable slices and each in half on a diagonal. Place each wrap on the plate for serving and fill up a sauce side dish with remaining sauce for dipping.

Empanadas

Empanadas are a fun way to use the tortillas in the wrap section of Simply Dehydrated, they are also a delight to serve and easy to save to enjoy all week long.

MAKES 4 TAPAS SERVINGS

For the filling:

2	cups soaked almonds
1	cup fresh corn
1	Roma tomato
½	cup water
4	Tbsp. extra virgin olive oil
2	Tbsp. chili powder
1	clove garlic
1	tsp. sea salt

For the wrap:

4	fresh Simple Tortillas (pg. 123)

To begin, place the finished wraps on a basic cutting board. Fill each with ¼ of the filling and gently fold over. Press the edges down with a fork until a nice pocket is formed. For added variation and texture, place in the dehydrator on a tray lined with a mesh screen at 118 degrees for 1-2 hours before enjoying. This will cause the filling to set and for the flavor to become more complex, while the exterior will form a firmer pocket. Enjoy fresh out of the dehydrator.

Simple Soups

This collection of recipes utilizes fresh produce that is simple and easy to use. These recipes can be in your dehydrator in minutes and enjoyed within the hour. For each recipe you will see suggested dehydrating times, however the principle of basic dehydrating works here, intensifying the flavors and further modifying the textures as these recipes are in the dehydrator. Your personal preference may be to leave them in longer or remove them before the suggested time frame; this is completely up to you. Enjoy!

Maitake Longevity Soup

Maitake mushrooms are known for their immune boosting abilities, and non-GMO cultured miso has been a part of healthy diets worldwide for centuries. This recipe incorporates a healthy dose of flavors from herbs, each with their own healing properties, and root vegetables, which are known for there physically grounding abilities.

MAKES 4 APPETIZER PORTIONS

For the broth:

1   zucchini

4   cups hot water

2   Tbsp. non-GMO miso paste
    (recommend red or white for
    best results)

1   clove garlic

1   green onion, stock and bulb

1   tsp. sea salt

1   Tbsp. chili powder (optional if
    you enjoy a spicier soup)

For the soup:

2   organic Maitake mushrooms,
    well cleaned

2   cups shredded carrots

2   stalks green onions

2   cloves minced garlic (optional)

4   Tbsp. sesame seeds, for garnish

1   cup fresh dulse or other
    seaweed, for garnish

Begin by combining the broth ingredients in a basic blender and blending on high until well combined. Then clean and prepare all soup ingredients and place them in a glass bowl, save the garnishes. Pour the broth over the soup ingredients into the glass bowl. Place the glass bowl into the dehydrator either on the bottom of the dehydrator or on a dehydration tray in the first slot at 125 degrees for 1-2 hours. The soup will not warm past 118 degrees in this time frame. Remove the soup and pour into pre-warmed bowls for best results and garnish as desired before serving. Leftovers may be saved for additional day in the refrigerator.

Carrot Ginger Soup

Carrot and ginger are the perfect combination to clean the blood, and strengthen and support the cardiovascular system. This delicious blend is also a fun option in the cold winter months, since ginger is a naturally warming herb.

MAKES 4 APPETIZER PORTIONS

For the soup:

1   large carrot

2   cups carrot juice

1   cup hot water

1   clove garlic

2   oz. ginger juice or 1 inch
     fresh ginger, peeled

1   tsp. sea salt

1   Tbsp. cumin

1   Tbsp. turmeric

½   cup cold pressed extra virgin
      olive oil

For the garnish:

½   cup Simple Sedona Flax
      Crackers (pg. 65)

4   oz. Walnut Crème

For Walnut Crème:

MAKES 1 CUP WALNUT CRÈME

1   cup walnuts

⅓   cup coconut water

⅓   cup young Thai coconut flesh

1   Tbsp. raw honey

½   tsp. cinnamon

1   tsp. sea salt

Begin by combining the soup ingredients in a basic blender, save the olive oil, and blend on high until well combined. Then while the blender is still on, add the olive oil until the mixture begins to emulsify, this technique will help keep the vegetable fibers from separating. Pour the soup ingredients into a glass bowl. Place the glass bowl into the dehydrator either on the bottom of the dehydrator or on a dehydration tray in the first slot at 125 degrees for 1-2 hours. The soup will not warm past 118 degrees in this time frame. Remove the soup and pour into pre-warmed bowls for best results and garnish as desired before serving. Leftovers may be saved for up to 3 additional days in the refrigerator.

For the Walnut Crème: Blend the nuts, coconut water, and thai coconut flesh until a thick puree forms. Add the remaining ingredients and puree until well combined.

Corn Chowder

This recipe is sure to warm your heart and keep you moving all throughout the year. It's a high protein version of a classic favorite you will love.

MAKES 8 APPETIZER PORTIONS

For the broth:

4   cups raw corn

2   cups hot water

1   cup raw cashews, pine nuts or macadamia nuts

¼   cup cold pressed extra virgin olive oil

1   clove garlic

1   green onion, stock and bulb

1   tsp. sea salt

1   Tbsp. chili powder

1   tsp. raw honey or
2 drops Stevia

2   Tbsp. nutritional yeast (optional)

For the soup:

2   cups raw corn

2   stalks green onions, diced

2   cups yellow squash, diced (optional)

½   cup Everyday Cheese (pg. 133) for garnish

Begin by combining the broth ingredients in a basic blender and blend on high until well combined. Then clean and prepare all soup ingredients and place them in a glass bowl, save the garnishes. Pour the broth over the soup ingredients into the glass bowl and toss both together. Place the glass bowl into the dehydrator either on the bottom of the dehydrator or on a dehydration tray in the first slot at 125 degrees for 1-2 hours. The soup will not warm past 118 degrees in this time frame. Remove the soup and pour into pre-warmed bowls for best results and garnish as desired before serving. Leftovers may be saved for 3 additional days.

Sedona Vegetable Chili

Chili is delicious as an appetizer or an entrée in itself. This recipe is easy to prepare and can be added to at the time of enjoyment with the rich flavors of avocado or olive!

MAKES 4 APPETIZER PORTIONS

For the broth:

1   zucchini

4   Roma tomatos

1   red bell pepper

1   chipotle pepper

2   cups hot water

1/8 cup onion, diced (red or white)

4   sun-dried tomato halves

2   cloves garlic

1   Tbsp. chili powder (optional
     to add more if you enjoy a
     spicier soup)

½   cup cold pressed extra virgin
     olive oil

For the soup:

2   cups Roma tomato, diced

2   cups yellow squash or zucchini,
     diced

2   cups cremini mushrooms, diced

4   Tbsp. green onions, diced,
     for garnish

4   Kale Crunchers (pg. 69)
     for garnish

4-8Tbsp. fresh avocado or diced
     olives, for garnish

Begin by combining the broth ingredients, save the olive oil, in a basic blender and blend on high until well combined. Then while the blender is on, add the olive oil until broth emulsifies. Prepare all soup ingredients and place them in a glass bowl, save the garnishes. Pour the broth over the soup ingredients into the glass bowl and toss until mixture is well dispersed. Place the glass bowl into the dehydrator either on the bottom of the dehydrator or on a dehydration tray in the first slot at 125 degrees for 1-2 hours. The soup will not warm past 118 degrees in this time frame. Remove the soup and pour into pre-warmed bowls for best results and garnish as desired before serving. Leftovers may be saved for 2 additional days in the refrigerator.

Marinated Vegetables

Marinated vegetables are a nice way to prepare vegetables, by maintaining the enzyme and nutritional value without having to use traditional cooking methods, which may create toxic by-products and begin to deplete the health aspects of your food. These variations are all prepared using the same method of creating a basic marinade and then coating vegetables with the marinade and placing them in the dehydrator. The longer they are in the dehydrator the softer and more flavorful the vegetables will become. However, at a certain point they will become too dry, for this reason we have included basic dehydrating times with the idea that you will enjoy these delicious combinations based on your own preference. To your health!

Asian Fusion Slaw

For the marinade:

1   cup extra virgin olive oil

⅓   cup coconut aminos, Bragg's aminos, Nama Shoyu or wheat-free Tamari

2   oz. ginger juice

1   Tbsp. miso paste

1   green onion

1   Tbsp. raw agave or raw honey

For the vegetable mixture:

2   cups shredded carrots

2   cups broccoli, chopped to a medium sized piece

2   cups sliced shiitake mushrooms

2   cups snap peas

4   Tbsp. sesame seeds (optional)

In a basic blender combine all marinade ingredients and blend well until a basic marinade is formed. This marinade can be also be used as a salad dressing or garnish, and will save for up to 4 days in the refrigerator.

Prepare the vegetable mixture by tossing all ingredients in a large sized mixing bowl. Top the mixture with marinade and toss until well coated. Once coated, let sit while you prepare your dehydration trays. Line 2 dehydration trays with your choice of non-stick drying surface over the mesh screens. Transfer the contents of the mixture onto the trays and spread out evenly over the two trays. Place the trays in the dehydrator at 118 degrees for 2-4 hours. Then remove the vegetables and enjoy warm. Store left overs in the refrigerator for up to 3 additional days, making sure to let cool before placing in the refrigerator.

Jenny's Favorite Mushroom Medley

MAKES 5 CUPS OF MEDLEY

For the marinade:

1   cup extra virgin olive oil
1   clove garlic
1   tsp. sea salt

For the vegetable mixture:

2   cups shiitake mushrooms, diced
2   cups portabella mushrooms,
    diced
2   cups maitake mushrooms, diced
4   cloves diced garlic

¼   cup fresh parsley or basil
    as garnish

In a basic blender combine all marinade ingredients and blend well until a basic marinade is formed. This marinade can also be used as a salad dressing or garnish, and will save for up to 4 days in the refrigerator.

Prepare the vegetable mixture by tossing all ingredients in a large sized mixing bowl. Top mushroom mixture with marinade and toss until well coated, mushrooms should absorb the moisture from the marinade. Once coated, let it sit while you prepare your dehydration trays. Line 2 trays with your choice of non-stick drying surface over the mesh screens. Transfer the contents of the mixture onto the trays and spread out evenly over the two trays. Place the trays in the dehydrator at 118 degrees for 1-2 ½ hours. Then remove the mushrooms and enjoy warm. Store left overs in the refrigerator for up to 3 additional days, making sure to let them cool before placing in the refrigerator.

Festive Beans

MAKES 4 CUPS OF FESTIVE BEANS

For the marinade:

1   cup extra virgin olive oil

3   Tbsp. orange juice

2   Tbsp. raw agave or raw honey

1   tsp. sea salt or miso paste

1   clove garlic

For the vegetable mixture:

4   cups green beans, yellow long
    beans or wax beans (French cut
    for best results)

1   cup tangerine slices

1   cup walnut pieces, soaked

In a basic blender combine all marinade ingredients and blend well until a basic marinade is formed. This marinade can also be used as a salad dressing or garnish, and will save for up to 4 days in the refrigerator.

Prepare the vegetable mixture by tossing all ingredients in a large sized mixing bowl. Top the vegetable mixture with marinade and toss until well coated. Once coated, let sit while you prepare your dehydration trays. Line 2 dehydration trays with your choice of non-stick drying surface over the mesh screens. Transfer the contents of the mixture onto the trays and spread out evenly over the two trays. Place the trays in the dehydrator at 118 degrees for 2-4 hours. Then remove the vegetables and enjoy warm. Store left overs in the refrigerator for up to 3 additional days, making sure to let cool before placing in the refrigerator.

118 Special Onions

MAKES 5 CUPS OF 118 SPECIAL ONIONS

For the marinade:

1   cup extra virgin olive oil

4   Tbsp. raw agave or raw honey

1   Tbsp. Himalayan salt

1   Tbsp. all seasoning blend

For the vegetable mixture:

2   cups red onions, sliced

2   cups yellow sweet onions, sliced

2   cups small broiler or pearl onions, sliced

In a basic blender combine all marinade ingredients and blend well until a basic marinade is formed. This marinade can also be used as a salad dressing or garnish, and will save for up to 4 days in the refrigerator.

Prepare the onion mixture by tossing all ingredients in a large sized mixing bowl. Top the onions with marinade and toss until well coated. Once coated, let sit while you prepare your dehydration trays. Line 2 dehydration trays with your choice of non-stick drying surface over the screens. Transfer the contents of the mixture onto the trays and spread out evenly over the two trays. Place the trays in the dehydrator at 118 degrees for 2-4 hours. Then remove the vegetables and enjoy warm. Store left overs in the refrigerator for up to 5 additional days, making sure to let cool before placing in the refrigerator. You may also let these dry all the way until a crispy garnish is formed. Once dry you can store in an airtight container and use indefinitely.

Everyday Vegetables

MAKES 8 CUPS OF VEGETABLES

For the marinade:

1   cup extra virgin olive oil

2   sun-dried tomatoes

2   cloves garlic

1   tsp. dehydrated onion

1   Tbsp. Italian seasoning

1   Tbsp. raw agave or raw honey
    (optional)

1   Tbsp. sea salt

For the vegetable mixture:

2   cups shredded carrots

2   cups red bell pepper, diced

2   cups yellow and green
    squash, diced

¼   cup sliced onions

2   Roma tomatos

2   Tbsp. Italian seasoning, dried

2   cups cauliflower (optional)

In a basic blender combine all marinade ingredients and blend well until a basic marinade is formed. This marinade can also be used as a salad dressing or garnish, and will save for up to 4 days in the refrigerator.

Prepare the vegetable mixture by tossing all ingredients in a large sized mixing bowl. Top the vegetable mixture with marinade and toss until well coated. Once coated, let sit while you prepare your dehydration trays. Line 3 dehydration trays with your choice of non-stick drying surface over the mesh screens. Transfer the contents of the mixture onto the trays and spread out evenly over the two trays. Place the trays in the dehydrator at 118 degrees for 2-4 hours. Then remove the vegetables and enjoy warm. Store left overs in the refrigerator for up to 3 additional days, making sure to let cool before placing in the refrigerator.

High Protein Marinated Vegetables

For the marinade:

1   cup extra virgin olive oil

1   red bell pepper

1   clove garlic

1   Tbsp. curry powder, chili
    powder, or ground basil

1   Tbsp. raw agave or raw honey

For the vegetable mixture:

2   cups shiitake mushrooms

2   cups red chard or lacinato kale,
    chopped

2   cups peas or green beans

2   cups walnuts, sprouted

In a basic blender combine all marinade ingredients and blend well until a basic marinade is formed. This marinade can also be used as a salad dressing or garnish, and will save for up to 4 days in the refrigerator.

Prepare the vegetable mixture by tossing all ingredients in a large sized mixing bowl. Top the high protein vegetables with marinade and toss until well coated. Once coated, let it sit while you prepare your dehydration tray. Line a dehydration tray with your choice of non-stick drying surface over a mesh screen. Transfer the contents of the mixture onto the tray and spread out evenly over the tray. Place the tray in the dehydrator at 118 degrees for 20 minutes-2 hours. Then remove the vegetables and enjoy warm. Store left overs in the refrigerator for up to 3 additional days, making sure to let cool before placing in the refrigerator.

Entrées

Entrées are a fun way to use the Sedona Dehydrator to create delicious dishes for the whole family. I have actually found that creating entrées using the dehydrator has been a great way to accomplish more in my day. In most cases I have already created the pantry staples I use in the dish so I just have some fresh preparation to do and then the assembly.

Once assembled most of the dishes go back into the dehydrator to warm and create additional flavors and textures. While the items are becoming culinary masterpieces, I am then free to take care of things around the house or run errands. When I am done I have a delicious dinner waiting for me!

The Sedona Dehydrator makes creating more culinary options for the living foods lifestyle a fun and easy process that saves time, eliminates toxic by-products created with high heat cooking, cuts back on waste and ultimately will leave me feeling healthy and refreshed.

Winter Squash Ravioli

Ravioli is one of my favorite entrée dishes, this is a savory option that is a great treat to enjoy during the winter months especially, but can also be made with sweet squash in the summer!

MAKES 4 ENTRÉE PORTIONS

For wrap:

1   tray of Simple Seed Wraps
    (pg. 116)

For the filling:

2   cups butternut squash

1   Roma tomato

$2/3$ cup water

4   Tbsp. olive oil

1   clove garlic

4   Tbsp. fresh rosemary

1   tsp. sea salt

To begin, in a high-power blender combine all filling ingredients and blend on high. Blend until a thick purée has formed. Once complete, transfer the filling to a dish. Line up the wrap on a cutting board, cut down into 2 inch by 4 inch rectangular pieces.

Line a dehydration tray with a mesh screen. Begin filling each piece of wrap with 2 full tablespoons of filling right in the center. Fold each wrap over onto itself and line up on the dehydration tray so the ravioli are not touching but still close to each other.

Place the dehydration tray in the dehydrator at 118 degrees for 4 hours, until the ravioli filling has set up. Serve this dish warm out of the dehydrator with your favorite marinara recipe for more flavors or alone. I love this dish with some fresh "Everyday Cheese" (pg. 133) sprinkled on the top. The leftovers may be refrigerated and saved an additional 2 days in an airtight container.

Fusion Pizza

Pizza is a nice hearty dish and this dish makes use of the high protein pizza crust featured in this book. We recommend using seasonal vegetables to spice up this dish all throughout the year. This pizza also looks lovely cut into triangles and served on appetizer platters.

MAKES 4 ENTRÉE PORTIONS

For crust:

4   Simply Dehydrated Pizza Crust
     (pg. 94)

For the filling:

2   cups seasonal vegetables
     (I prefer heirloom tomato,
     marinated squashes, and
     mushrooms in combination)
1   cup Everyday Cheese (fresh
     before dehydrating- pg.133)
1   cup fresh basil finely chopped
4   Tbsp. olive oil
1   clove garlic, diced
1   tsp. sea salt

To begin, in a basic mid-sized bowl for mixing toss together vegetables, oil, diced garlic, chopped basil and sea salt. Toss until well combined. Layer each pizza crust with ¼ cup of "Everyday Cheese" and top with ½ cup of fresh vegetable mixture.

Line 2 dehydration trays with mesh screens. Place completed pizzas on the screen, 2 per screen.

Place the dehydration trays in the dehydrator at 118 degrees for 1 hour, until the cheese has begun to set and the vegetables have softened and warmed. Serve this dish warm out of the dehydrator and garnish with additional fresh herbs or dried garnishes. Leftover pizza may be refrigerated and re-warmed for up to 3 days.

Tangy Thai Bowl

Thai flavors are known for their warming abilities in the body and this mixture is a great example of how to combine multiple components from the Sedona Dehydrator for in-depth culinary dishes in your kitchen.

MAKES 4 ENTRÉE PORTIONS

For topping:

2   cups of Firecracker Crisps
    (pg. 136)

For the bowl basic set-up:

4   cups Asian Fusion Slaw
    (pg. 164)

4-8 cups kelp noodles, squash
    noodles or steamed quinoa

For the Thai Sauce:

4   Tbsp. almond butter

1   Tbsp. raw honey or raw
    agave nectar

1   green onion, bottom white
    portion only

1   Thai pepper (optional)

1   tsp. sea salt

Juice of 1 lime

To begin use your personal blender, or a basic immersion blender to make the Thai sauce, by combining the basic ingredients and blending well. This sauce will last up to 7 days in the refrigerator and can be made in advance to help with weekly menu planning.

In a basic mixing bowl, toss the slaw and your choice of bowl base. Here you may choose a completely raw option or a transitional item like steamed quinoa. It is up to you how much of the base you'd like to enjoy in comparison to the slaw, I recommend equal parts as outlined in the recipe. After tossing well, divide the mixture into 4 even portions and plate or place in a bowl. Top each portion with a drizzle of the Thai Sauce.

Place the bowls in the dehydrator at 118 degrees for 1 hour for a more intense flavor and to warm the dish further if preferred. Serve this dish warm out of the dehydrator with an additional spritz of lime.

Dim Sum Dumplings

I love this dish! It is a delicious and delicate dish that awakens the palate and brings a rich sense of nourishment at the same time. This dish can be prepared in advance and stored for enjoyment throughout the week as well.

MAKES 3 ENTRÉE PORTIONS

For wrap:

1   tray of Sushi Wraps (pg. 122)

For the filling:

2   cups Mushroom Medley (pg. 166)

2   cups Sweet Onions (pg. 58)

2   cups chopped Napa cabbage

For the filling base:

1   cup pine nuts, macadamia nuts or cashews

⅓   cup water

2   Tbsp. olive oil

2   Tbsp. raw agave or raw honey

1   tsp. sea salt or 1 Tbsp. coconut aminos

Juice of 1 lime or 1 oz. ginger juice

To begin, in a personal blender or other basic blender, combine all filling base ingredients and blend on high. Blend until a thick purée has formed. Once complete, transfer the filling to a dish. Line up the wrap on a cutting board, cut down into 3 inch squares.

Line a dehydration tray with a mesh screen. Begin filling each piece of wrap with 3 full tablespoons of filling base right in the center. Toss all filling ingredients together so that the marinades from the vegetables coat the nappa cabbage in a mid-sized mixing bowl. Top the filling base with 4 Tbsp. of filling mixture. Fold each wrap into the center, pinching all four corners together to form the dumplings. Then place each dumpling on the dehydration tray so the dumplings are not touching but still close to each other. Refrigerate additional filling ingredients.

Place the dehydration tray in the dehydrator at 118 degrees for 4 hours, until the dumpling filling has set up. Serve this dish warm out of the dehydrator with the remaining fresh filling ingredients on the bottom of the plate (remove these vegetables from the refrigerator about 1 hour before enjoying and let warm to room temperature). The leftovers may be refrigerated and saved an additional 2 days in an airtight container.

Spinach Quiche with Walnut Crust

Quiche is easy to make in larger batches and you can enjoy it all week long. This is a very popular dish at catering events and even for morning enjoyment. The nuts are an essential oil the brain uses for immediate nourishment and the topping is high in protein.

MAKES 8 ENTRÉE PORTIONS

For crust:

1   tray of Nutty Bread
    (use half way through drying
    process- pg. 88)

For the topping:

4   cups spinach

½   cup red bell peppers, sliced

2   cups butternut squash

1   Roma tomato

⅔   cup water

4   Tbsp. olive oil

4   Tbsp. flax seeds

1   clove garlic

4   Tbsp. fresh rosemary

1   tsp. sea salt

To begin, in a high-power blender combine all topping ingredients, save spinach and red bell peppers, and blend on high. Blend until a thick purée has formed. Once complete, transfer the topping to a dish. Toss into the bowl the spinach and red bell peppers. Let it sit a few moments for mixture to thicken.

Line a dehydration tray with a mesh screen. Place the bread crust on the tray over the mesh screen and then evenly spread over the quiche topping. Spread the topping out evenly on the crust.

Place the dehydration tray in the dehydrator at 118 degrees for 4 hours, until the quiche topping has set up. Serve this dish warm out of the dehydrator with your favorite marinara recipe for more flavors or alone. The leftovers may be refrigerated and saved an additional 3 days in an airtight container.

Ranchito Wrap

Ranchito wraps were inspired by the simplicity of ranch style living, garnished with the hearty nature of staying connected to the land we call home. Ranchito wraps are a meal in themselves or may be cut in half to serve alongside a fresh seasonal salad.

MAKES 4 ENTRÉE PORTIONS

For wrap:

1   tray of Simple Seed Wraps (pg. 116) or Simple Tortillas (pg. 123)

For the filling:

2   cups fresh shredded carrots

2   cups chopped spinach or nappa cabbage

1   avocado, diced

3   fresh tomatos, diced

¼   cup green onions, diced

1   diced Jalapeno or Anaheim pepper (optional)

For the ranchito sauce:

1   Roma tomato

1   red bell pepper

½   cup almond milk

4   Tbsp. olive oil

4   Tbsp. chili powder

Juice from 1 lemon

To begin, in a personal blender combine all ranchito sauce ingredients and blend on high. Blend until a purée has formed. Once complete, transfer the sauce to a mid-sized mixing bowl and add all filling ingredients. Toss the sauce and the filling ingredients well. Line up the wrap on a cutting board, cut down into 4 rectangular pieces, or choose 4 tortillas.

Line a dehydration tray with a mesh screen. Begin filling each piece of wrap with ¼ of filling down the center. Roll each wrap around the filling and line up on the dehydration tray.

Place the dehydration tray in the dehydrator at 118 degrees for 1 hour, until the wrap has warmed and the vegetables have softened slightly. Serve this dish warm out of the dehydrator with any additional sauce over the top or additional avocado or guacamole on top. Leftovers may be saved in an airtight container in the refrigerator for up to 2 days. It is recommended to dry the leftovers at 118 degrees for ½ hour to an hour before enjoying.

Risotto

Risotto can be accomplished quickly and easily in the Sedona dehydrator using sprouted grains, quinoa, or squash pieces. Enjoy this dish with friends on a lazy Sunday afternoon.

MAKES 4 ENTRÉE PORTIONS

For Risotto Base:

4 cups sprouted kamut or wheat berries, 4 cups finely diced zucchini, or 4 cups steamed quinoa

4 cups Mushroom Medley (pg. 166)

2 cups Everyday Vegetables (pg. 169)

For the Risotto Sauce:

2 cups macadamia nuts or cashews

2 Roma tomatos

1 cup water

4 Tbsp. olive oil

1 clove garlic

4 Tbsp. lemon juice

2 Tbsp. dried Italian herbs or 118 Spice Blend (pg. 137)

1 tsp. sea salt

To begin, in a high-powered blender combine all sauce ingredients and blend on high. Blend until a thick purée has formed. Once complete, transfer the sauce to a large mixing bowl and add in the risotto base ingredients. Fold in all ingredients until well combined.

Line a dehydration tray with a mesh screen and your choice of non-stick sheet. Transfer risotto to the tray and press out to create an even layer.

Place the dehydration tray in the dehydrator at 118 degrees for 1-2 hours, until mixture has softened. You should smell a delicious aroma circulating in your kitchen. Serve this dish warm out of the dehydrator. Garnish with fresh herbs or "Everyday Cheese" (pg. 133). The leftovers may be refrigerated and saved an additional 2 days in an airtight container.

Divine Pasta

20 minutes or less is all this delicious dish takes, and it is a delicious bowl of pasta to be enjoyed any time of the year.

MAKES 4 ENTRÉE PORTIONS

For the pasta:

6   cups julienned squash noodles (zucchini or yellow crookneck works best)

For the sauce:

1   cup pine nuts, cashews or macadamia nuts

3   Roma tomatoes

2/3 cup water

2   Tbsp. nutritional yeast (optional)

4   Tbsp. olive oil

1   clove garlic

4   leaves fresh basil

1   tsp. sea salt

For the topping:

2   cups seasonal produce, finely chopped (cauliflower, mushrooms, and heirloom tomato are my favorite to incorporate into this dish)

To begin, in a personal blender combine all sauce ingredients and blend on high. Blend until a thick puree has formed. Once complete, transfer the filling to a mid-sized mixing bowl. Combine in the bowl all ingredients and toss well.

Line a dehydration tray with a mesh screen and your choice of non-stick drying sheet. Transfer the pasta onto the tray and dehydrate at 125 degrees for 20-40 minutes to soften noodles.

Seasonal Sedona Sandwich

Sandwiches are a delicious way to enjoy fresh breads and other dehydrated goodies like marinated vegetables from the Sedona Raw Foods Dehydrator. These are also easy to travel with and make a great addition to any lunchbox!

MAKES 4 ENTRÉE PORTIONS

For the bread:

1   tray Simple Sprouted Bread
     (pg. 80)

For the filling:

2   Hass avocado

4   leaves of fresh chard

1   heirloom tomato or 1 red bell
     pepper, thinly sliced

1   cup of Marinated Vegetables of
     choice (pg. 170)

Juice of 1 lemon

Assembly: Line up the bread on a cutting board and cut into 8 even pieces, either rectangular or in triangles.

In a small mixing bowl smash the avocado, lemon juice and sea salt. Line each piece of bread with some of this avocado mixture to begin assembly. Then layer ½ of the slices with a piece of chard, followed by the tomato or red bell pepper, top this with the marinated vegetables and finish with remaining bread pieces.

You may choose to dehydrate these sandwiches for a warm sandwich, to accomplish this simply place on a dehydration tray lined with a basic screen and place in dehydrator at 125 degrees for ½ hour. This will warm the sandwich before serving.

Desserts

Desserts! Everyone loves a great dessert, especially a fresh, flavorful option that is also healthy. This collection of desserts makes use of some of the best features of the Sedona Raw Food Dehydrator. Since everyone has a sweet tooth, they are also a great way to introduce family and friends to remarkable living foods creations that will surely tantalize their taste buds.

Desserts can be modified as well to fit what you have in your own garden that is fresh and in-season. These recipes and techniques are a guide to help you create some culinary magic of your own, so get playful with it and enjoy these tasty treats.

Blackberry Pie

Blackberries provide a delicious burst of flavor as well as a great source of antioxidants. When combined in this delicious recipe, you can be sure of a decadent dessert that will delight the most discriminating of pie connoisseurs.

MAKES 5 ONE INCH SLICES OF PIE

For the crust:

2   cups walnuts

⅓   cup raw agave nectar or
     raw honey

2   Tbsp. lemon zest

1   Tbsp. coconut flour (optional)

1   tsp. sea salt

For the topping:

4   cups fresh blackberries

⅓   cup raw agave nectar or
     raw honey

In a basic food processor with the s-blade in place process the nuts from the crust into a basic meal. Add in the lemon zest, coconut flour and salt and pulse until well combined. Then add the desired sweetener while the machine is in operation. A crust or dough ball should begin to form. Turn off the food processor at this point.

In a small bowl, place the blackberries and additional sweetener of choice. Gently smash the blackberries so that some are broken down and some remain whole and full of body.

Line a dehydration tray with a mesh screen and a non-stick drying sheet of your choice. Then transfer dough ingredients onto the dehydration tray and form a 5 inch round, or line a glass 5 inch pie dish. Then pour over the topping ingredients and evenly spread over crust.

Once completely assembled place dehydration tray in the dehydrator set at 118 degrees. Dehydrate at 118 degrees for 2 hours until the pie has softened and the berries have sweetened. Serve warm and refrigerate leftovers for up to a week.

Pumpkin Spice Bars

Pumpkin Spice Bars are a delicious treat and a great way to use fresh pumpkin. They can be prepared in advance and enjoyed all week long or made fresh on the spot. Enjoy yours with a warm glass of chai tea and really get your taste buds dancing!

MAKES 8-10 BARS

For the crust:

2   cups walnuts or pecans
½   cup raw agave nectar or
     raw honey
1   Tbsp. cinnamon
1   Tbsp. maca root (optional)
1   tsp. pumpkin pie spice
1   tsp. sea salt

For the topping:

4   cups fresh pumpkin, diced
1   cup raw agave nectar or
     raw honey
2   Tbsp. almond butter
⅔   cup fresh water
4   Tbsp. flax seeds or chia seeds
1   oz. ginger juice (optional)
1   tsp. sea salt

In a basic blender combine all topping ingredients and blend very well until a thick paste has formed. Chill this mixture while preparing crust. In a basic food processor with the s-blade in place process the nuts from the crust into a basic meal. Add in the spices and pulse until well combined. Then add the desired sweetener while the machine is in operation. A crust or dough ball should begin to form. Turn off the food processor at this point.

Line a dehydration tray with a mesh screen and a non-stick drying sheet of your choice. Then transfer dough ingredients onto the dehydration tray or into a 6 by 8 inch glass baking dish. Press the dough out flat in a 6 by 8 inch shape flat. Then pour over the topping ingredients and evenly spread over crust.

Once completely assembled place dehydration tray in the dehydrator set at 118 degrees. Dehydrate at 118 degrees for 4-5 hours until the pumpkin has set up, and the flavors have intensified. Serve warm and refrigerate leftovers for up to a week. For best results I recommend cutting down into bar size desired, prior to storing.

Persimmon Bars

Persimmons are a delicious and nutritious food option offering a variety of essential daily vitamins and a great soft texture and sweet flavor. Fuyu persimmons are optimal for this dish and can create a fantastic dish the whole family is sure to enjoy.

MAKES 8-10 BARS

For the crust:

2   cups pecans

½   cup coconut flour or
    buckwheat flour

½   cup raw agave nectar or
    raw honey

1   Tbsp. cinnamon

1   tsp. nutmeg

1   tsp. sea salt

For the topping:

4   cups persimmons, thinly sliced
    and cut on a bias

1   cup raw agave nectar or
    raw honey

2   Tbsp. cinnamon

1   tsp. sea salt

In a basic food processor with the s-blade in place process the nuts from the crust into a basic meal. Add in the spices and pulse until well combined. Then add the desired sweetener while the machine is in operation. A crust or dough ball should begin to form. Turn off the food processor once dough ball forms.

Line a dehydration tray with a mesh screen and a non-stick drying sheet of your choice. Then transfer dough ingredients onto the dehydration tray or into a 6 by 8 inch glass, baking dish. Press the dough out flat in a 6 by 8 inch shape flat. Toss topping ingredients together in a mid-sized mixing bowl. Then pour over the topping ingredients and evenly spread over crust.

Once completely assembled place dehydration tray in the dehydrator set at 118 degrees. Dehydrate at 118 degrees for 3 hours until the persimmons have softened. Serve warm and refrigerate leftovers for up to a week. For best results I recommend cutting down into bar size desired prior to storing.

Toffee Bars with Goji Berries

Toffee Bars are a Sunday Brunch favorite and a top seller on our daily dessert menu at 118. We hope you love them as much as we do!

MAKES 12-16 BARS

For the bar base:

4   cups pecans

2   cups raw cacao

1   cup cup raw agave nectar or raw honey

1   Tbsp. cinnamon

1   tsp. sea salt

For the topping:

1   cup almonds

1   cup goji berries

1   cup espresso beans (optional, replace with cacao nibs if preferred)

½   cup coconut butter

½   cup raw cacao

⅓   cup raw agave nectar or raw honey

1   tsp. sea salt

In a basic food processor with the s-blade in place process the nuts from the base into a basic meal. Add in the cacao and spices and pulse until well combined. Then add the desired sweetener while the machine is in operation. A crust or dough ball should begin to form. Turn off food processor once dough ball is formed.

Line a dehydration tray with a mesh screen and a non-stick drying sheet of your choice. Then transfer dough ingredients onto the dehydration tray and press out evenly to cover the tray.

Then in a mid-sized bowl whisk together the cacao, sweetener of choice, and sea salt until well combined. Using an offset spatula spread out this mixture over the bar base. Then in the food processor with the s-blade attachment in place pulse the remaining topping ingredients until chopped down to smaller pieces. Take this topping and sprinkle over the bars.

Once completely assembled place dehydration tray in the dehydrator set at 118 degrees. Dehydrate at 118 degrees for 2 hours until the toffee bar has become cake like. Serve warm or freeze and serve cold. Store leftovers for up to 21 days in the refrigerator.

Fig Crust with Orange Marmalade

Fig Crust with Orange Marmalade is a very versatile and low glycemic dish that is a fabulous late afternoon snack, dessert or even breakfast. Figs are very high in potassium and also contain protein.

MAKES 12 FIG CRUSTS WITH ORANGE MARMALADE

For the crust:

3   cups soaked mission figs, or fresh mission figs

½   cup walnuts

4   Tbsp. yacon syrup, raw agave nectar or raw honey

1   Tbsp. cinnamon

1   vanilla bean or ½ tsp. vanilla paste

1   tsp. sea salt

For the topping:

4   cups oranges (blood oranges are awesome in this dish as well), diced, with seeds removed

4   Tbsp. orange zest

2   Tbsp. almond butter, walnut butter, cashew butter or coconut butter

1   tsp. sea salt

In a mid-sized mixing bowl whisk together topping ingredients. Then, in a basic food processor with the s-blade in place process the nuts from the crust into a basic meal. Add in the remaining crust ingredients and process until well combined and a dough ball begins to form.

Line 2 dehydration trays with mesh screens and a non-stick drying sheet of your choice. Then scoop out fig crust onto the sheet in 4 Tbsp. sections across the first screen. Press each down so a round shape is formed that is ½ inch thick. Take the other tray and line with the topping mixture in the center of the tray.

Place both trays in the dehydrator and set the dehydrator at 118 degrees. Dehydrate for 2 hours. Then take the marmalade topping and place on the top of the crusts, evenly dividing it over the crusts. Place the crusts back in the dehydrator at 118 degrees for 1 additional hour.

Remove the crusts and serve warm. Leftover crusts will save for an additional 10 days in an airtight container, when refrigerated.

Almond Biscotti

Biscotti is a delicious option for serving with tea and is a nice, high-energy, high-protein way to enjoy a sweet treat. This simple recipe is easy to create and can be saved indefinitely for ongoing enjoyment! This recipe is easy to double as well.

MAKES 12 BISCOTTIS

- 2 cups soaked almonds or almond meal
- 2 cups ground raw buckwheat flour
- ¾ cup raw agave nectar or raw honey
- 1 Tbsp. cinnamon
- 1 tsp. sea salt

In a basic food processor with the s-blade in place add the almonds and the sweetener and process until well broken down and combined. Add the buckwheat flour and spices and process to dough.

Line a dehydration tray with a mesh screen and a non-stick drying sheet of your choice. Then transfer dough ingredients onto the dehydration tray. Press the dough into a 4 by 6 inch square ¾ of an inch thick.

Place dehydration trays in the dehydrator and set at 118 degrees, then dehydrate for 4-5 hours until the bar is firm. Flip over and score biscotti, cutting down into lengthwise strips ½ inch wide. Dehydrate again, for an additional 8 hours, until completely dry but still a bit soft. Store in an airtight container in your pantry.

Cinnamon Raisin Cookies

Delicious cookies, good when served warm and incredible with fresh almond milk! Kids love these dessert treats as well. One trick is to make them half size so they are easy to hold by hands of all ages!

MAKES 12-18 COOKIES

- 2 **cups walnuts or pecans, soaked**
- 2 **cups raisins, soaked**
- 4 **Tbsp. raw honey, coconut nectar or agave**
- 1 **Tbsp. cinnamon**
- 1 **tsp. nutmeg**
- 1 **tsp. sea salt**

In a basic food processor with the s-blade in place add all the ingredients and process to rich cookie dough.

Line 2 dehydration trays with mesh screens and a non-stick drying sheet of your choice. Scoop out dough 1-2 Tbsp. at a time, lining up cookies across the tray so they are close but not touching. Press the dough down into round cookie shapes.

Place dehydration trays in the dehydrator set at 118 degrees and dehydrate at 118 degrees for 6 hours until the cookies are completely dry. They should naturally be a bit soft but not sticky at all. Flip over half way through and place directly on dehydration screens to shorten drying time.

Gingerbread Cookies with Coconut Sugar

Coconut sugar is a fun ingredient to enjoy sparingly, it makes a fabulous holiday cookie, but these cookies can be repurposed as ginger snaps all year long using different cookie cutter shapes.

MAKES 10-12 GINGERBREAD PEOPLE

3   cups pecans
1   cup coconut flour
½   cup coconut sugar (optional, use extra pecans if you prefer to leave it out)
½   cup water
1   Tbsp. cinnamon
1   oz. ginger juice or 1 tsp. ground dried ginger
1   tsp. nutmeg
1   tsp. sea salt

In a basic food processor with the s-blade in place, add all the ingredients and process to rich cookie dough.

Line 2 dehydration trays with mesh screens and a non-stick drying sheet of your choice. Transfer cookie dough to non-stick sheets and roll out using a rolling pin ¼ inch thick. Using cookie cutters create gingerbread people, re-using the dough in-between until all of the dough is used.

Place dehydration trays in the dehydrator set at 118 degrees and for 6 hours until the cookies are completely dry. They should naturally be a bit soft but not sticky at all. Flip over half way through and place directly on dehydration screens to shorten drying time.

Creamy Caramel Torte

Creamy Caramel Tortes are another delicious torte, I like to make both the spirulina tortes and the caramel tortes and serve them together on a dessert tray. They make a stunning visual appeal and the flavors and texture is a nice compliment to one another.

MAKES 6-12 TORTES

Basic Savory Crust (pg. 203):

2   cups walnuts

1   red bell pepper, diced

2   Tbsp. olive oil

1   Tbsp. Italian seasoning

1   clove garlic

1   tsp. sea salt

For the topping:

1   cup coconut butter or young
    Thai coconut flesh

2   bananas

⅓   cup raw yacon syrup, agave
    nectar or raw honey

1   Tbsp. vanilla paste or natural
    vanilla flavor

2   Tbsp. maca root or Lucama
    powder

2   Tbsp. cinnamon

1   tsp. nutmeg

1   tsp. ground dried ginger

1   tsp. sea salt

First prepare torte crusts in advance. Line a torte mold with saran wrap or parchment and press dough in to fill. Remove dough once molded into shape.

Line a dehydration tray with a mesh screen and your choice of non-stick sheet. Line up torte crusts across sheet until complete. Place the dehydration tray in the dehydrator at 118 degrees for 4-6 hours until completely dry and cake-like. Store in an airtight container away from light until ready to use. Makes 6-12 torte crusts depending on size of mold.

Then when ready, blend topping ingredients in basic blender. Scoop mixture onto torte crust and freeze entire torte for 1 hour prior to serving. Tortes should be kept in freezer until ready to enjoy and can be enjoyed for up to 7 days from first preparation.

Spirulina Torte

Simple yet, fun to look at and even more fun to eat, tortes are a great way to enjoy the Sedona Raw Food Dehydrator. Make a batch of torte crusts to top at a moment's notice.

MAKES 6-12 TORTES

Basic Savory Crust:

2   cups walnuts

1   red bell pepper, diced

2   Tbsp. olive oil

1   Tbsp. Italian seasoning

1   clove garlic

1   tsp. sea salt

For the topping:

4   fresh bananas or 2 avocados

4   Tbsp. raw agave or raw honey

1   Tbsp. vanilla paste or natural vanilla flavor

4   Tbsp. spirulina or other greens powder

1   tsp. sea salt

For Basic Savory Crust: In a basic food processor with the s-blade attachment in place process first the walnuts down to a meal. Then add in the remaining ingredients, save the oil and process until well combined. Finally add the oil and process until a dough ball forms. Remove crust and store in the refrigerator in an airtight container until ready to prepare your entrée.

First prepare torte crusts in advance. Line a torte mold with saran wrap or parchment and press dough in to fill. Remove dough once molded into shape.

Line a dehydration tray with a mesh screen and your choice of non-stick sheet. Line up torte crusts across sheet until complete. Place the dehydration tray in the dehydrator at 118 degrees for 4-6 hours until completely dry and cake-like. Store in an airtight container away from light until ready to use. Makes 6-12 torte crusts depending on size of mold.

Then when ready, blend topping ingredients in basic blender. Scoop mixture onto torte crust and freeze entire torte for 1 hour prior to serving. Tortes should be kept in freezer until ready to enjoy and can be enjoyed for up to 7 days from first preparation.

Cacao Bites

Cacao Bites are the third torte option. You may choose to use carob in place of cacao. These delightful treats were inspired by my grandmother Ross and her annual holiday baking. Fun for the eyes and the taste buds, this variation makes an excellent introduction to living cuisine for curious friends and I like to keep a batch out on the counter-tops to keep inspired healthy living flowing in our home.

MAKES 6-12 CACAO BITES

Basic Savory Crust (pg. 203):

2   **cups walnuts**

1   **red bell pepper, diced**

2   **Tbsp. olive oil**

1   **Tbsp. Italian seasoning**

1   **clove garlic**

1   **tsp. sea salt**

For the topping:

1   **cup raw cacao**

½   **cup coconut butter or young Thai coconut flesh**

4   **Tbsp. raw agave or raw honey**

1   **Tbsp. vanilla paste or natural vanilla flavor**

1   **Tbsp. cinnamon**

1   **tsp. sea salt**

1   **drop essential peppermint oil (optional variation)**

First prepare torte crusts in advance. Line a torte mold with saran wrap or parchment and press dough in to fill. Remove dough once molded into shape.

Line a dehydration tray with a mesh screen and your choice of non-stick sheet. Line up torte crusts across sheet until complete. Place the dehydration tray in the dehydrator at 118 degrees for 4-6 hours until completely dry and cake-like. Store in an airtight container away from light until ready to use. Makes 6-12 torte crusts depending on size of mold.

Then when ready to prepare, blend topping ingredients in basic blender. Scoop mixture onto torte crust and freeze entire torte for 1 hour prior to serving. Tortes should be kept in freezer until ready to enjoy and can be enjoyed for up to 7 days from first preparation.

Mango Coconut Crème Pie

Tropical flavors combine in this delicious frozen pie. Use your Sedona Raw Food Dehydrator to make up this delicious basic pie crust in advance and your pantry will be ready at a moments notice to entertain friends. We recommend serving this pie frozen for ease of serving, but it is also delicious as a breakfast topped with fresh fruits and super foods.

MAKES 6 ONE INCH SLICES OF PIE

Simple Pie Crust:

4   cups raw walnuts

¾   cup raw agave nectar, ½ cup
     raw dates or ½ cup raw honey

2   Tbsp. orange zest (optional)

1   tsp. sea salt

Pie filling:

2   cups fresh mango

1   cup pineapple

1   cup fresh young Thai coconut

1   Tbsp. raw coconut butter or
     more coconut flesh

2   Tbsp. raw agave nectar or
     raw honey

Begin by preparing a pie crust in advance. First set up the food processor with the s-blade attachment in place. Then add in the nuts and process to a basic meal, being careful not to let it go too long so that butter forms. Add in desired spices and then process, while processing add desired sweetener from the top of the food processor while processing until dough ball forms.

Line a dehydration tray with a mesh screen and non-stick sheet of your choice. Remove dough from food processor and place on dehydration tray. Press crust out to a 6 inch round about ½ inch thick. If you'd like you can also create a lip around the pie or create small pie crusts. Another option is to fill a glass pie pan and press pie crust into pan, placing the entire dish into the dehydrator to dry.

Set the dehydrator at 118 degrees and dry pie crust for 6-8 hours, so that desired texture is reached. The crust should be dry to the touch. Store crust in an airtight container until ready to fill.

Then blend pie filling ingredients in basic blender until a rich thick pie filling is formed. Place the filling inside the crust and freeze for 2-4 hours before serving.

Pecan Pie

This is a rich and decadent recipe, a little bit goes a long way with this pie and it is sure to satisfy as the end to any flavorful meal.

MAKES 6 ONE INCH SLICES OF PIE

Simple Pie crust:

4   cups raw pecans

¾   cup raw agave nectar, ½ cup raw dates or ½ cup raw honey

2   Tbsp. orange zest (optional)

1   tsp. sea salt

Pie filling:

1   cup pecan butter

2   bananas

2   Tbsp. raw agave nectar or raw honey

1   Tbsp. cinnamon

1   tsp. nutmeg

1   tsp. sea salt

1   cup pecan pieces (for garnish)

Begin by preparing a pie crust in advance. First set up the food processor with the s-blade attachment in place. Then add in the nuts and process to a basic meal, being careful not to let it go too long, so that butter forms. Add in desired spices and process. While processing add desired sweetener from the top until dough ball forms.

Line a dehydration tray with a mesh screen and non-stick sheet of your choice. Remove dough from food processor and place on dehydration tray. Press crust out to a 6 inch round about ½ inch thick. If you'd like, you can also create a lip around the pie or create small pie crusts. Another option is to fill a glass pie pan and press the pie crust into pan, placing the entire dish into the dehydrator to dry.

Set the dehydrator at 118 degrees and dry pie crust for 6-8 hours, so that desired texture is reached. The crust should be dry to the touch. Store crust in an airtight container until ready to fill.

Then blend pie filling ingredients, save garnish in basic blender until a rich thick pie filling is formed. Place the filling inside the crust and freeze for 2-4 hours before serving. Garnish with fresh pecan pieces and serve chilled.

Chocolate Lava Cake

Lava cake may seem like a tricky recipe the first time you prepare it but rest assured you will love it once you get the hang of it. This is a rich and creamy cake best served warm and dripping with the lava filling and some fresh berries.

MAKES 8 CAKES

For the cake:

3 cups raw pecans

1 cup raw cacao

½ cup raw agave nectar or raw honey

2 Tbsp. raw cacao butter or coconut butter

1 Tbsp. cinnamon

1 tsp. sea salt

For the lava filling:

1 cup raw cacao powder

½ cup coconut oil or coconut butter

⅛ cup raw agave nectar

1 tsp. vanilla paste

1 tsp. cinnamon

1 tsp. sea salt

6 strawberries, diced (optional)

Begin by preparing the crust in the food processor with the s-blade attachment in place. Process the nuts down to a meal. Add in all further ingredients until rich dough is formed.

Then in a basic personal blender, combine all filling ingredients and blend well. (If you are using the strawberries, fold them in with the basic lava filling, in a mid-sized mixing bowl.)

Line a dehydration tray with mesh screen and your choice of non-stick drying sheet. Then scoop out 1 Tbsp. of dough and line up 8 cakes across the dehydration tray. Press the dough out to form a base for the cake into rounds about 1/8 inch thick across tray. Then scoop out another 2 Tbsp. of cake and form a ring around the top of the base on each cake. Fill each ring with 2 Tbsp. of lava filling.

Place dehydration tray in the dehydrator and dry at 118 degrees for 2-4 hours. The cakes should be moist and the filling should thicken and warm. Top with any additional sauce and serve warm. Refrigerate leftovers for up to 7 additional days.

Almond Butter Fudge Bars

"Delicious gooey goodness" is all I can say about this bar, you will love it! I love these bars straight out of the dehydrator, but they are also good chilled. I make these in advance so I can enjoy them all week long.

MAKES ROUGHLY 8 BARS

For the crust:

4   cups Almond Biscotti cookie
      dough (pg. 199)

For the topping:

2   cups raw almond butter
2   cups Chocolate Lava Cake
      filling (pg. 211)
4   Tbsp. cinnamon (for garnish)
**Fresh chopped banana (for garnish
at time of serving)**

Line a dehydration tray with a mesh screen and your choice of non-stick sheet. Press out cookie dough into a ½ inch layer across the dehydration tray. Using an offset spatula spread over the almond butter evenly over this first layer. Then pour over the chocolate layer.

Place the dehydration tray in the dehydrator at 118 degrees for 3 hours. Serve warm and soft, garnished with fresh cinnamon and banana.

Buttery Walnut Cookies

Buttery Walnut Cookies are an elegant cookie, perfect for a tea party or afternoon soirée. They have a great crunch while still being a nice soft cookie and are universally enjoyed by crowds of all backgrounds.

MAKES 12-18 COOKIES

For the cookie:

2   cups soaked walnuts
½   cup raw dates
1   Tbsp. cinnamon
1   tsp. nutmeg
1   tsp. sea salt

For the topping:
1 ½ cups Buttery Walnuts (pg. 102)

In a basic food processor with the s-blade in place add all the ingredients and process until rich cookie dough is formed that is close to nut butter in texture.

Line 2 dehydration trays with mesh screens and a non-stick drying sheet of your choice. Scoop out dough 2 Tbsp. at a time, lining up cookies across the tray so they are close but not touching. Press the dough down into round cookie shapes and using the back of a fork score the cookies. Then place some "Buttery Walnuts" on top of each cookie, pressing them down into the dough.

Place dehydration trays in the dehydrator set at 118 degrees and dehydrate at 118 degrees for 4-6 hours until the cookies are completely dry. They should naturally be a bit soft but not sticky at all. Flip over half way through and place directly on dehydration screens to shorten drying time.

Avocado Crème Bars

Avocado is an unlikely ingredient in desserts, however avocado makes a nice rich, gelato type topping when combined properly and placed to chill. This is a great dessert to finish any luncheon and stays vibrant in color for up to a week.

MAKES 8 BARS

For the bar:

4   cups Simple Pie Crust (pg. 206)

For the topping:

4   fresh Hass avocado (medium)

1   cup coconut water

½   cup raw agave or raw honey

4   Tbsp. orange juice

1   tsp. sea salt

2   Tbsp. orange zest (garnish)

Begin by preparing the crust. Line a dehydration tray with a mesh screen and your choice of non-stick drying sheet. Press out the pie crust onto the tray to cover the tray at ¼ inch in thickness. Place the dehydration tray in the dehydrator and dry the crust at 118 degrees for 4-6 hours.

Meanwhile blend the topping ingredients (save garnish) and chill. Once the crust is dry to the touch, remove it from the dehydrator and let cool. Spread over avocado topping in an even layer and serve fresh or freeze for 1 hour before serving. This dish should be kept refrigerated and can be enjoyed for up to 5 days after first preparation.

Cookie Cut Outs

Stars, hearts, x's and o's, any shape can be accomplished with this basic cookie. Enjoy making this cookie with kids of all ages.

MAKES 12-18 COOKIES

For the cookie dough:

2   cups macadamia nuts

2   cups coconut flour

4   Tbsp. coconut butter or 2 Tbsp. coconut oil

⅔ cup raw agave or raw honey

1   Tbsp. vanilla paste or vanilla bean

1   tsp. sea salt

For the glaze:

½ cup raw agave nectar or raw honey

1   Tbsp. cinnamon

1   dash sea salt

In a basic food processor with the s-blade in place add all the cookie dough ingredients and process until a dough ball forms.

Line 2 dehydration trays with mesh screens and a non-stick drying sheet of your choice. Scoop out dough onto cutting board lined with non-stick surface and use cookie cutters to create shapes no thicker than ¼ inch in thickness. Place cookies on dehydration tray so they cover tray but do not overlap. In a small mixing bowl whisk together glaze ingredients and brush glaze onto cookies.

Place dehydration trays in the dehydrator set at 118 degrees for 6 hours, until the cookies are completely dry. They should naturally be a bit soft but not sticky at all. Flip over half way through and place directly on dehydration screens to shorten drying time.

Honey Date Squares

Honey Date Squares are easy to pack, to travel with, and are a high protein snack. Enjoy them as a dessert, high energy snack, breakfast or while on your next backpacking trip.

MAKES 9 HONEY DATE SQUARES

2   cups almond butter or tahini
2   cups fresh dates, pits removed
⅓   cup coconut shreds
4   Tbsp. raw honey
4   Tbsp. fresh orange zest
4   Tbsp. poppy seeds
1   vanilla bean- inside only (optional)
2   Tbsp. hemp seeds
1   Tbsp. sea salt
(Add super foods as desired)

In a basic food processor set up with the s-blade in place process all ingredients until well combined. There will still be chunks of each ingredient but they should hold together nicely when combined.

Line a dehydration tray with a mesh screen and your choice of non-stick drying surface. Transfer dough onto sheet and press out into a 6 by 6 inch square. Gently cut down further to 2 by 2 inch squares. Place in the dehydrator at 118 degrees for 4-6 hours until completely dry, yet still soft enough to easily bite through. To shorten drying time you may want to transfer the squares straight onto the tray at 1 hour into the drying time.

Afterword

In closing, I'd like to take a moment to remind you that it may take some time to fully realize all the benefits of switching from cooking in an oven to dehydrating. As you create all different types of delicious recipes, you will learn the ins and outs of this simple machine and find incredible freedom in your kitchen!

The benefit of committing to this process can immediately be seen in terms of healthy and vibrant living. Using all the great fresh fruits, vegetables, seeds, sprouted grains and nuts, that are readily available in your kitchen, to make incredible dishes will leave you feeling empowered and, overall, offer you tremendous health benefits.

The Sedona Raw Food Dehydrator allows you to create foods that are free from the harmful side-effects of high temperature cooking and create snacks that are high in enzymes and still contain their nutritional value. It will also provide you freedom from harmful food additives and synthetics in your food.

In addition, the Sedona Raw Food Dehydrator will also provide you with time saving abilities and allow you to prepare fantastic plant-strong dishes using your own creations! Getting back into the kitchen is a fun and empowering way to take back your health and open the doors to limitless possibilities!

To your vibrant health!

Peace and Blessings,

Chef Jenny Ross

About the Author

Chef Jenny Ross, the owner and executive chef of the living-foods restaurants, 118 Degrees, in Orange County, California, has been a pioneering spirit of the raw-foods movement since 2000, beginning with her first Los Angeles café. As a chef, her unique creations have captivated customers nationwide, and her product line is available in health-food stores throughout the country. Jenny travels and educates on the healing properties of living foods and the benefits of the living foods lifestyle.

Jenny works with clients of all backgrounds, motivating them toward more vibrant health while teaching them about the healing power of living foods. Her award-winning cuisine has drawn a celebrity clientele to her restaurant and has been a positive catalyst for changing many lives.

Please visit her website:
www.118degrees.com
www.jennyrosslivingfoods.com

Recipe
Index

FRUITS & VEGETABLES

OLIVES AND OILS

Stevia

Resources

FOR THE SEDONA DEHYDRATOR:

U.S. Distributors

Tribest Corporation
1143 N. Patt St.
Anaheim, CA 92801
Phone: 714.879.7150 or 888.254.7336
www.tribestlife.com
Manufacturer and main distributor of the Sedona Dehydrator.

A+B Health Wholesale
95 Golden Hill Rd.
Danbury, CT 06811
Phone: 203.748.9966
Fax: 201.427.9031
US distributor for the Sedona Dehydrator and other healthcare products.

Healthwise
3800 Happy Lane, Suite A
Sacramento, CA 95827
Phone: 916.463.0171
Fax: 916.463.0176
US distributor for the Sedona Dehydrator and other healthcare products.

Midwest Health Supply
21355 Highway 179
Jamestown, MO 65046
Phone: 660.849.2133
Fax: 660.849.2134
www.vitalityplus1.com
US distributor for the Sedona Dehydrator and other healthcare products.

International Distributors

Alpha Health Products Ltd.
7434 Fraser Park Drive
Burnaby, B.C. V5J 5B9 Canada
Phone: 604-436-0545 or 800-663-2212
Fax: 604-435-4862
www.alphahealth.ca
Canadian distributor for the Sedona Dehydrator, as well as other health equipment for the kitchen.

Keimling Naturkost GMBH
Zum Fruchthof 7A
21614 Buxtehude
Germany
Phone: +49 4161 5116 135
Fax: 49-4161-5116-272
www.keimling.de
German distributor for the Sedona Dehydrator, as well as other health equipment for the kitchen.

Raw Pleasure
20 Johns Road
Mudgeeraba QLD 4213
Australia
Phone: 1-800-729-838
Fax: 604-435-4862
www.raw-pleasure.com.au
Australian distributor for the Sedona Dehydrator and other healthcare products.

Savant Distribution Ltd.
Quarry House
Clayton Wood Close
Leeds LS16 6QE United Kingdom
Phone: 44-113-230-1993
Fax: 44-113-388-5238
www.savant-health.com
UK distributor for the Sedona Dehydrator, as well as other health equipment for the kitchen.

Vitajuice Showroom & Eko Cafe
02-797 Warsaw
Al. KEN 21 lok. U1
Poland
Phone: +48 22 224 67 39
Service: +48 502 195 000
www.vitajuice.pl
Polish distributor for the Sedona Dehydrator, as well as other health equipment for the kitchen.

RECOMMENDED READINGS:

The Art of Raw Living Food by Doreen Virtue and Jenny Ross

Living with Green Star by Elysa Markowitz

Raw Gourmet by Nomi Shannon

Ani's Raw Food Desserts by Ani Phyo

Raw Basics by Jenny Ross

Raw Food Made Easy by Jennifer Cornbleet